SURVIVAL
GUIDE
FOR THE
NEW
MILLENNIUM

To Dona,
Be Prepared,
Syp Richmond

Survival Guide
for the
New Millennium

How to Survive the Coming
Earth Changes

BYRON KIRKWOOD

BLUE DOLPHIN

1993

For further information address
Blue Dolphin Publishing, Inc.
P.O. Box 1908, Nevada City, CA 95959

ISBN: 0-931892-54-6
First printing: January, 1993

Library of Congress Cataloging-in-Publication Data

Kirkwood, Byron.
   Survival guide for the new millenium : how to survive the coming earth
changes / Byron Kirkwood.
     p. cm.
   Includes bibliographical references.
   ISBN 0-931892-54-6 (pbk.) : $8.95
    1. Mary, Blessed Virgin, Saint (Spirit)—Prophecies—Miscellanea.
   2. Twentieth century—Forecasts.   3. Survival skills—Miscellanea.
   I. Kirkwood, Byron. II. Title.
   BF1311.M42K57 1992
   133.9'3—dc20   92-41591
                                     CIP

Printed in the United States of America by
Blue Dolphin Press, Grass Valley, California

5   4   3   2   1

Dedication

I WANT TO THANK MY WONDERFUL WIFE, Annie, for her part in assisting and encouraging me in this venture. I also appreciate the help in proofreading, encouragement and suggestions from our friends, as well as the following people and groups for their contribution to this survival guide: Gordon-Michael Scallion of the Matrix Institute, the wonderful people of Sparrow Hawk Village in Oklahoma, Debby Cody, and Barbara Brewer.

This work is dedicated ultimately to those destined to inherit the earth.

Preface

THIS SURVIVAL GUIDE IS INTENDED TO GET YOU THINKING. In some ways it is only a primer, a sourcebook to direct you to other information that covers particular subjects in greater depth.

After starting this project I found there are a lot of good books that cover survival basics and techniques. I also found that the subject of survival means different things to different people. To some people "survival" means going out into the woods and eating roots. To others it seems to involve war games— weapons and an enemy.

Survival to us means to prepare to handle the upcoming earth changes and live to see the beginning of the next millennium. It means that we are preparing to be self-reliant. We cannot wait for the "government" to take care of us, but need to be able to help not only ourselves, but as many others as possible.

—B.K.

Table of Contents

Introduction

THIS IS A GUIDE TO HELP YOU SURVIVE the coming crises which are predicted to happen over the next few years. For those who do not know about these crises, here is an abbreviated explanation.

The planet Earth is going through a "rebirth" or rejuvenation. There is an incredibly huge wave of energy coming through space towards the Earth, like nothing the planet has ever experienced. At the peak of the passing of this wave, the Earth will literally turn on its axis and there will be new North and South poles. There will be a new equator, and land and water masses will change. After the energy wave passes, our entire solar system will have moved to another location in the galaxy. Another sun will enter our solar system and stay, and we will become a binary system. This event has been foreseen for over 2000 years. It is the "end time" that was foretold in the *Book of Revelation*. It is often called the upcoming "Earth Changes," and it is the predecessor to the "Thousand Years of Peace."

My wife, Annie Kirkwood, is the receiver of *Mary's Message to the World* (Blue Dolphin, 1991), a message sent to Annie through her mind by Mary, Mother of Jesus. As "God so loved the world that he sent his only begotten son . . .", Mary so loves the people of this planet that she is warning us of the impending crises. *Mary's Message* has ten chapters. Only one of these, Chapter 2, is devoted to Mary's predictions. The predictions are not the main message; the main message is to return to God. *Mary's Message* is intended to help us prepare spiritually for the upcoming events.

Chapter 2, "Mary's Predictions" was given to add credibility to her message, to draw attention to the impending situation, **and to give us time to prepare.** In this chapter Mary warns us and gives specific dates by years of events that will unfold. For the detailed predictions I suggest you read *Mary's Message to the World.* Key predictions include increasingly larger storms, tornados, huge floods, volcanic activity, earthquakes and the eventual turning of the Earth on its axis in 1999. Mary is quick to state, "Make sure you understand that this is not the end, but the beginning of a new era and a new world and a new understanding. The need to prepare is now, before the birth of a new era."[1]

Mary's Message awoke me to what is happening. However, this rebirth has been predicted by many modern day psychics and prophets, including Edgar Cayce, Ruth Montgomery, Gordon-Michael Scallion and Lori Wilkins. These events have been predicted by the Hopi Indian prophesies for over 10,000 years. It is the time spoken about in every civilization's folklore.

As mentioned earlier, this is the end time referred to in the *Book of Revelation.* Chapter 10 of *Mary's Message,* "A Message from Jesus" explains the *Book of Revelation* in modern terms. Revelation was written in "allegory and riddle." According to the information contained in *Mary's Message,* Jesus says, "John did not have the words to describe the future. He did not have a word for the destruction which the atomic bomb would cause. He did not know how to describe the dumping of chemical waste. No one had heard of chemicals. No one knew about

---

[1]*Mary's Message* (MM), chapter 2, page 20.

these kinds of waste. So John told as best he could those events as they were shown to him."[2]

Whether you actually believe that these events will happen or not is not extremely important. What *is* important is that you keep an open mind as the events unfold. If the message is true, the events will make believers of us. Even the closed minded will have to wonder what is happening when the ground is shaking over the entire planet, the weatherman is telling of "the largest storm . . . ever," and lava is forcing people to leave their homes. The clincher will be if, and when, a major part of California returns to the sea in 1995 (or before).[3]

Gordon-Michael Scallion, a modern-day prophet, sees California as the "Isles of California." He predicts that this will occur sometime between September and December 1995.[4]

When this happens it will be time to take the predictions seriously. In many ways it will even be too late, because **it won't be business as usual after this happens**. But for the die-hard, doubting Thomas, it will be time to start acting, instead of just reacting.

It is understandable that these predictions will cause fear in many people. **That is not the intent!** The intent is to start people thinking about the things they should be doing *now*, to prepare to survive this event. A certain kind of fear is helpful. We are told,

> Fear is an alarm, a signal that something needs your attention. Fear in this instance tells you to move, run, hide, and/or protect yourself and your loved ones. Fear in this light then is good. It is much like noise. Noise is used as an alarm, a warning device. Noise is not pleasant, nor is it good for a prolonged period of time. Likewise, fear is not good for you if it is in your

---

[2]MM, chapter 10, pages 174-75.
[3]From MM, page 14. The "or before" refers to other predictions that California may suffer the big one as early as 1993.
[4]The Earth Changes Report (ECR) by Gordon-Michael Scallion, volume 2.4, May 1, 1992, page 3.

life for a prolonged time. What is fear telling you? It is saying, you are in danger, look and act. . . . Trust in your own innate abilities. They were placed there in the beginning to protect and guide you. . . . The time is fast approaching when you will have only your trust and beliefs to guide you. All people will be in uncharted territory. The world will be dealing with unusual feelings from the energy wave, unusual circumstances and unusual climate. You will feel that you have suddenly been transported to another world.[5]

For those who already believe this *is* happening and *will* happen, this book is for you—to help you prepare for the physical survival. For those that don't yet believe, but don't want to be caught unprepared, it is also for you. For those that refuse to believe, buy it and put it on the shelf, where you can find it when the radio or television announcer breaks in with an announcement, "California has just suffered a major earthquake measuring. . . ."

My inner guidance has led me to write this book—to help people start planning, to take some sort of action. In reviewing *Mary's Message*, I read that Mary gave us her message and the predictions "for those who believe to have time to prepare for these events" and that "Mary is very concerned for both the spiritual well-being of mankind and for its **physical well-being.**"[6] This is my contribution, to help with the physical survival of mankind through these coming, trying times.

I hope that these events never happen and that the rest of my natural life is business as usual. And at worst, if I am labelled a "kook or quack," it is after-the-fact. But this is not what I believe, and Annie and I are beginning our preparation, both physically and spiritually. *Mary's Message* (and many other sources) will help with the spiritual preparation. This book is intended to help with the physical preparation for those of us destined to survive to the beginning of the third millennium.

---

[5] Annie continues to receive messages from the spirit world. They are guiding us with words and thoughts. This came from one such message.
[6] MM, page 6.

1

Overview

IF YOU SURVIVED THE INTRODUCTION to this point, I assume you accept that these events will occur, or at least have some likelihood. Therefore, I am going to use the predictions that have been given by *Mary's Message*, Gordon-Michael Scallion, Edgar Cayce, Ruth Montgomery, and others, as if they will indeed happen. There are probably a lot of minor differences, but I'll use the common parts to try to shape a picture of what will be happening in the future. This is to allow us to prepare for these events as best we can.

I do not want to duplicate the material that is in *Mary's Message*, but I will mention enough about it that someone that hasn't read it can understand what is meant.

As I convey this information I will mention that "we are/were told" or "received," referring to information we have been given from the spirit world, usually by the Brotherhood. This is the Brotherhood of God, also known as the White Brotherhood or the Holy Ghost. It doesn't matter if you believe that this form of communication is possible or not. What is truth, and important to you, will strike a nerve as you read it.

Background

Since *Mary's Message* has been published, Annie and I have been getting the feeling that we will be moving. We are now calling these feelings, "being guided." Where we will move and under what circumstances, we don't know. We sensed, and now accept, that it will be a rural or farm area. Now this is strange, for both of us are city folks. I was born in Dallas and Annie in Fort Worth, Texas. We've lived around here all our lives, except for a short stay in Utah, while working for a company based there. My only contact with a farm or rural environment was as a child, when I visited my grandmother in the Texas panhandle. My dim memory recalls that I may have milked a cow and gathered a few eggs while visiting my grandmother. But this is the extent of my farming experience. Whether our move is to an individual farm or to a community of like-minded people, we don't know as yet.

We are also been guided in other ways. Early this year (1992), I kept sensing that I should get back into electronics and amateur radio. As a teenager I got interested in ham radio and got my amateur license. Then I got married, had children, started my own business, and eventually lost interest in hamming (amateur radio). I let my call (license) expire and sold off my equipment. Then I got the idea that I should get back into radio. Annie and I were visiting a Radio Shack electronics store one Sunday when I spotted their amateur radio license manuals. I bought the manual on a Sunday, started preparing, and took and passed the test for Technician Plus (the 3rd level in amateur radio) the next Saturday. I have since upgraded two more levels to Advanced Class (there is only one level higher). I even passed the dreaded 13 words-per-minute of Morse code, something I hadn't been able to accomplish as a youngster. **I feel I was being guided to ham radio, because independent radio communications will be very important in the future**. Amateur radio is currently enjoying a resurgence in popularity.[1] It would be vain and stupid to think that we are the only one's being guided.

The point to this step-by-step guided scenario of my amateur radio experience, is to suggest that you let your instincts guide you! To quote Gordon-Michael Scallion, "I would strongly suggest everyone listen carefully to their intuition, dreams, feelings, etc, and follow their guidance for what they should do. . . ."[2]

The interest in amateur radio led to the next area of concern. How will radios be powered during and after major catastrophes, when power is disrupted or power systems fail completely? Batteries will eventually run down and gasoline will be in short supply. This led me to think about using solar power as a source of electricity.

A strange event happened when Annie and I visited a used book store. I was in search of material on solar cells, looking in the area designated for electronics and electrical books and finding nothing. A store clerk bent down to pick up a box of books. I asked her if she had anything on solar power? She said "wait a minute" and went to the back of the store and dug through a pile of used books. She uncovered a book called *Producing Your Own Power*.[3] This turned out to be an excellent primer on all forms of alternative power sources: wind, water, wood, methane, and solar power (but ironically not solar cells). It is a 1976 vintage book, but it has made an excellent primer.

It seems the more I get interested in and start learning, the more my need to learn grows. Since getting interested in alter-

---

[1]For those that have been curious about getting into amateur radio, but have been put off by the code requirement, you can now get an amateur license without learning code. It is the "no code" Technician class license that allows you VHF (Very High Frequency) and UHF (Ultra High Frequency) privileges. All you have to do is read a study guide and take a test. The importance of amateur radio, during and after the earth turning is not that you have a license, but by that time you should be knowledgeable and have the equipment on hand.

[2]ECR, volume 2.4, May 1, 1992, page 4.

[3]*Producing Your Own Power—How to Make Nature's Energy Sources Work for You* edited by Carol Hupping Stoner, Rodale Press, sixth printing, Sept. 1975.

native sources of energy, I am also developing interest in other subjects such as hydroponics and welding. There is probably a pattern here, in that all these skills or areas of knowledge will be useful in coming times.

The Safe Areas

I mentioned that Annie and I were being guided to move our residence. One of the most popular questions that Annie and other psychics are asked is, "where is a safe area" or "is xxx a safe area?" Over and over again we are told that we will be guided to a safe area, if we develop our own internal connection to God; that the answer will come to us through our minds. Or, as Gordon-Michael Scallion mentions, follow your intuition, dreams and feelings.

In discussing "safe" areas we need to look at several definitions of what we mean by "safe." After the Earth turns some areas that have been above ground will be under water. These are not safe areas. Other areas that have been under water will rise, but will not be ready for habitation for many years. In some sense, no area is safe, in that all areas will experience major disasters due to the huge storms, tornados, floods, lightning, mudslides, earthquakes, volcanoes, and other events that will happen. Mother Mary tells us, "What I say is that all parts of the globe will be affected. Every nation and every area of this world will feel the storms and the turmoil."[4] So a safe area may be one that experiences less damage and turmoil than most. Being beneath a mountain range may not be safe until after the planet stabilizes from the polar shift. Boulders will be shaken loose during the giant earthquakes and mudslides will occur where there is excessive rain.

---

[4]MM, page 26.

One aid to moving to a "safe area", or at least an area above water, may be the map of the U.S. after the turning, developed by and available through psychic Lori Wilkins of "I Am America."[5] This shows how Lori sees America after the turning. I noticed that Dallas becomes a sea port, while Houston is under water. Her map shows only a small part of California above water and it is indeed an island. Gordon-Michael Scallion released his "The Future Map of the United States," at the Global Sciences Congress on August 15th, 1992. Gordon's map is similar but there are some noticeable differences. One such difference is that the United States is completely divided by an inland ocean where the Mississippi River was previously. The price of his map is $12.00 including postage and handling.

We've asked about particular areas and we have been given general answers. Obviously California, or most of California, is not a safe area. It seems that the central part of the U.S. is safest after the earth stabilizes. The coastal areas are not considered safe. Near any large body of water is not safe. This apparently includes large lakes, but not small streams or ponds. In the mountains may not be safe when the giant earthquakes happen. But high ground between mountains may be safe, if far enough away that the mountains (large boulders, etc.) wouldn't fall on you.

There is another issue relative to safe areas. The riot in Los Angeles in late April, 1992, is but a preview of what can result when a major catastrophe happens. Gordon-Michael Scallion even foresaw these riots and is predicting more riots in 1993.[6]

In a message Annie received, we were told, "Many are being led to leave the cities for many reasons. 1. As the earth moves those who are steeped in fear will react in violence. You do not want to be here for that. 2. As the earth moves and storms come, the fearful will feel extremes of fear and it will

---

[5]"I AM AMERICA, P.O. Box 2511, Payson, AZ 85547, cost $15 plus $3.00 postage and handling.
[6]ECR, volume 2.4, May 1, 1992, page 1.

come out not only in violence, but in anarchy and those who are there to protect will be part of the violence and anarchy." Can you grasp the significance of this?

The Alien Connection

For those who have read *Mary's Message,* or are current on the upcoming events, you may be aware that a rescue mission has been in the planning stages for hundreds or even thousands of years. This is an organized effort by the inhabitants of the other worlds, the space brothers, aliens, or extraterrestrials, as we sometimes call them. This too has been foretold for ages. Apparently the ancient Mayans or Incas even foretold the year of the return as our year 2024. I consider this pretty close, considering everything. Many groups are looking to this rescue mission and/or an ascension for their survival. It may be, for some! One well-meaning person even told me not to worry about all this "survival stuff," because we would be taken care of (by the space brothers). If this is true, we still need to survive the storms and other events that will happen between now and the rescue.

I have asked about the rescue mission and was told this was indeed being implemented. But that no one, except our higher self, knows what is in their individual life plan. I have even asked the Brotherhood how many will survive the turning, how many will be taken off the planet, and how many will return to the spirit world (not survive the turning). I was told that an estimated two-thirds of the earth's population will die the physical death and return to spirit, before or as a result of the turning. Of the one-third that is left, some will be taken off the planet by the space brothers. I was specifically reminded that no one knows who will be taken, who will return to spirit, and who will be left on earth to survive.

Summary

I spoke at a recent seminar and was asked, "When the turning happens . . . wouldn't we be taken care of? Why should we do all this (preparation)?" I answered by telling a story I heard a few years ago that seemed very appropriate. It goes something like this:

> "There was a man in a house and it was flooding outside. A neighbor came by and said 'we need to evacuate.' The man answered, 'No! God is going to take care of me.' The water continued to rise and the man was forced upstairs. Others came by in a boat and offered to rescue him. He told them, 'No! God is going to take care of me.' Finally the man is up on the roof of his house and a helicopter arrives to offer help. Again the man says, 'No! God is going to take care of me.' Finally the water consumes the man and he drowns.
>
> "He goes to heaven and is presented before God. He complains to God, 'I thought you were going to take care of me!' God answers, 'I sent you a neighbor, a boat and a helicopter, what more did you need?'"

I think someone is trying to tell us something! Maybe we should prepare for survival on earth. This is what this book is all about—preparing to survive on planet Earth up to and after the turning.

CHAPTER

2

The Three Periods

THE NEAR FUTURE CAN BE DIVIDED INTO THREE PERIODS, as it pertains to survival and the coming events. Please remember that I am stating the predictions as if they will definitely occur. I obviously hope this is not the case. However, my beliefs are strong enough that I am writing this book to help you prepare. Perhaps the best way to read this is to imagine it as a part you are playing in a movie. Like a movie actor, you have to understand the script and get into the role. If you don't think of it like this, it will probably overwhelm you and cause panic, fear and inaction.

The PREPARATION Time

The first period is the time of PREPARATION. **This is the most crucial period of all!** This period is between now (1992) and the beginning of a breakdown in our normal society. The breakdown in the United States may begin as soon as the end of 1995, when California is predicted to return to the ocean, or as late as 1999, when the planet is predicted to turn on its axis.

Our country will feel the effect of the loss of California more than other parts of the world. However, the turning will definitely affect every part of the globe. So the exact end of the Preparation time and the beginning of the next period will be relative to where you are located on the planet.

When a major portion of California breaks off from this continent, things will no longer be normal in this country. This will be a reference point for the entire world, warning of what is in store for the planet.

Have you ever thought about the interdependence of our modern day society? Try to imagine what day-to-day business will be like when California sinks into the ocean. The financial system would quickly shut down. Within a few days you won't be able to cash a check, especially if it is written on a California bank. With this kind of panic, bank runs will occur, and banks would soon shut their doors to prevent being forced out of business.

A major portion of our food supplies come from California. How long do you think food stuffs will exist on your local grocer's shelves after a panic run to stock up? Electronic equipment suppliers would be virtually out of business, after their inventory runs out. Most of the semiconductor components are manufactured or sourced in California. Just about every piece of modern equipment contains electronics as a key element. Today's cars cannot be fixed without electronic equipment. And often a car's "computerized" component has to be replaced. What I am trying to say is, no part of our society would be untouched as a result of the California catastrophe!

Then there is the human element. How many lives would be touched? Most of us have family or friends in California. How about those of us that don't live there, but might be there on a vacation or business trip when this happens? All this will affect our lives—it will not be business as usual.

After this happens, things will eventually start to settle down and it may appear to return to normal. But it will never reach a normal condition, as it was prior to this event. The economic system will begin to deteriorate up to the time of the turning. During the time between the California catastrophe and the turning there are still the other major catastrophes to be reckoned with, those caused by huge storms, earthquakes and volcanoes all over the world. These too will take their toll on our lives.

I don't want to belabor these points, but these are the predictions. All this has been predicted as far back as Nostradamus in the sixteenth century, and by every modern-day prophet or psychic I am aware of. And yet, very few people are doing anything to prepare for this event, especially those people living in California.

The SURVIVAL Time

The next period I call the SURVIVAL time. This is the time between the breakdown of normal civilization and about twenty years after the turning. This is the time for which this book is intended to help you prepare. But the opportunity to prepare is during the Preparation time. This book will have little or no value to anyone waiting to read it after the turning, except maybe to support saying, "I told you so."

The Survival era will begin as a time of desperation, especially for those that haven't made any preparations. It will be worse in larger cities. People with guns will take from those that have supplies, especially food, clothing, and gasoline, just to name a few. And fear and panic will cause people to do crazy things. The Los Angeles riots in April, 1992, gave us a preview of what the larger cities will be like during this desperate time. The difference is that everyone that is hungry will be trying to get enough to feed themselves and their families. It will be a time of chaos and anarchy.

In rural and farm areas where people are more capable of becoming self-sufficient, it will not be as bad. The further these are from major cities, the better. It wouldn't be long before those in the cities leave to try to find better living conditions.

When and where a minimum level of civilization is obtained, bartering will become the standard method of exchange, so those with an abundance of items will trade for other needed or desired items. As the confusion and chaos subside, services will also be bartered for necessities. Paper money, checks, and credit cards will all be worthless. Some coins and precious metals such as gold may still be taken as a medium of exchange in some locations. But the real valuables will be food, medical supplies, and other hard goods. The magazine *Practical Survival* is quoted: "**After a collapse, people who rely on anything from government will do without.**"[1]

The key to preparing for this time is to consider what planning, skills, items, property and materials are needed to assist in surviving. This is the basis for the next chapter.

The AFTERTIME

Sometime approximately twenty years after the turning of the planet on its axis, we will enter the AFTERTIME. This will be the beginning of the "Thousand Years of Peace." In the Aftertime we will have developed a new culture. The shock of the planet's turning will implant a new value system on our lives. A new standard of civilization will begin to develop. We will again become self-sufficient. New technologies will develop for living.

This time is better described in Chapter 9, "The Aftertime" of *Mary's Message*. The goal of the survival effort is to help those intended to make it to this time. I hope all those who desire and prepare make it to this era.

---

[1]*Practical Survival,* article titled "Barter: Currency for Troubled Economies" by V. R. Farb, June/July 1992, pages 20-22.

The NATURAL PREPAREDNESS

Simultaneously with and during the Preparation time, we must prepare for major disasters that will be happening. These are huge storms, tornados, hurricanes, mudslides, earthquakes, volcanoes, fierce lightning storms, and such. They will all play havoc with our society's systems of emergency aid, medical, insurance, banking, food and water distribution.

Preparation for these events will be somewhat different than the long range preparedness that is needed for the Survival time. This is a short range, immediate preparedness. Although this is what our Civil Defense program prepares for, we cannot rely on others for this. We must individually prepare for these events. We are calling it "Natural Preparedness," to prepare for the natural events that will be happening.

When the major disasters happen, you won't be able to dial "911" and have an ambulance arrive and have everything taken care of. There won't be enough ambulances, fire trucks, and paramedics to handle the entire community at once. We must become "self-reliant." We must plan on handling these situations as best we can.

Those that are prepared spiritually and physically will have an added advantage. They won't be as likely to panic and do dumb things, simply because they are panicking.

The Three Days of Darkness

This is not an era such as the Preparation, Survival and Aftertimes. However, it is a critical time that must be prepared for. It happens at the time of the turning of the planet on its axis. This event has been predicted and you will need to plan for the **three days of darkness**. Much volcanic debris, gases and other substances will be in the air at the time of the turning. It will block out the sun for at least three days or more—some psychics are predicting a darkening up to at least a year or more—and the air outside will not be breathable without special apparatus. During this time lightning will do strange things, such as enter into buildings. Electrical, electronic and magnetic devices may not work. The Earth's gravity may be out of balance.

When I'm told that Earth's gravity will be out of balance, I envision people flying up into the air to eventually wind up in outer space. I am told that this is not the case, as the wind will come down from the sky and hold everything down. This doesn't make sense to me, but it's what I've been told. I have learned that there are a lot of things that don't make sense, until the time comes when it happens. This is a rambling way of saying, "just accept it on faith!" If this doesn't happen, then it doesn't matter. If it does happen, some bright person will later explain it in a "logical or scientific" manner.

After I started this section on the three days of darkness, I was referred to *Rolling Thunder—The Coming Earth Changes* by J. R. Jochmans, a book which covers the earth changes in detail. In a section titled "The Three Days of Unknown Death," the messages of several psychics and visionaries are combined describing the three days of darkness. This section emphasizes some of the things that I mentioned above, which include: the air will contain noxious fumes and because of this people will drop dead on the spot. Lightning will go amok destroying many buildings and people. Air will be pulled from the atmosphere. One prophet predicts that only "one-fourth" of mankind will survive. A modern psychic, Criswell, of California, even gives the date of this event as August 18, 1999. This date is consistent with information Annie received, that the turning will be between the third and ninth months of 1999.

In the next chapter on "Preparing for the Survival Time" I will discuss how to prepare for the "three days of darkness."

CHAPTER

3

Preparing for the Survival Time

PROBABLY THE BEST WAY TO PREPARE is to imagine that you are going to move to a completely isolated island and then burn the boat. The boat is big enough to carry everything you might want to bring with you to live as pleasantly as possible the rest of your natural life, and enough to start future generations off right.

To start off we will need an initial stock of food, enough to last until we can get another source established. This could mean that we are going to grow our future food supply, or be able to hunt for meat and other naturally provided items. If we are going to grow our food, we will want to stock our boat with all the variety of seeds we will need. We will also need the tools to farm and cultivate the land. We may include fertilizer and how-to-farm books, if we are learning this the hard way.

Next we are going to need shelter and clothes. Clothes will eventually wear out, so we will need a way to replace the worn ones. I'll let you take it from here. By now you should have the idea of the process to think through.

How well you prepare is a function of how much time and money you put into the effort. If it's a matter of loading up the car to leave the city in a few minutes, that's one scenario. If you start in 1993 and have until at least 1995, that's a better situation and you should be better prepared. If you have this much time, you will have probably established a new residence and laid in a supply of crucial items.

Now back to reality

We can consider preparing for three possible levels of survival. These are based on your own choices: commitment to the task, how much time you have left to prepare, and the financial resources you are willing to commit.

These levels are:

1. The bare minimal existence: the things that are important are water, food, shelter, medical supplies and those items to maintain health and a minimum level of security.
2. Mid-range existence: you will have prepared and have an adequate amount of water, food and supplies to be able to survive. You will barter to trade items and services you possess for items you need.
3. High-level of existence: this can be accomplished if there is a high level of resources and planning invested in the effort. This might include "renewable forms of energy" that allow you to use many of the "modern" conveniences and maintain a reasonable high standard of living. You will likely have established a new residence and food could be home grown.

Let's assume that we recognized the need to prepare in time to really do it up right. What should we start doing now, today, while life's normal?

The Plan

First is an awareness that **you need a plan**. Do you stay where you are, or do you move to another location? If you can afford it, you might have a second residence. It might be considered a summer home, lake house (see safe areas), or any other justification for the place of refuge. This place should be located in a safe area, whatever that means to you personally.

Are you going to move there permanently? If so, does your financial situation require employment? What are you going to do for income (money) while things are still normal?

If the move is not a permanent one, what is going to signal the time to leave your permanent residence and take up residence in the secondary location? How are you going to get there? It is probably going to require driving, to transport the last of the items you need to take with you. If it is too late in the crises, you wouldn't be able to fly on a commercial airline to your location. If you drive, you can't depend on gas stations being open, having gas, or if they do—what form of payment will they be willing to accept? So the plan should involve having extra gas. This might be in gas cans, but they are dangerous. If you planned far enough ahead, you might have an auxiliary gas tank installed in your vehicle. Selecting the vehicle might be important for those that plan ahead.

Your plan should include how to rendezvous with other family members that may join you at your safe house.

These are all things you need to plan for to increase your chances of surviving.

The skills you will need

Consider what knowledge or skills you need to survive. These are areas that you should **start learning about now.** No one can be expected to know everything, but you should at least attempt to learn the basics of as many of the important skills as possible.

Farming, or the growing of at least a minimum amount of food, is on the top of my list. Until things begin to normalize (maybe five years after the turning), you can't depend on anyone except yourself and your family for your food supply. After times normalize you may be able to trade for food.

I've started my study in farming with hydroponics, the growing of foods out of the soil. In hydroponics nutrients are supplied by water. Many books are available covering this topic. I also read about "composting" in which waste is recycled into nutrient rich fertilizer. Methane gas is also created from waste materials.

When I first started thinking about our survival, I "assumed" that energy, mainly electricity, was out of the question. Why? Because most of the electric production and delivery system will be shut down, for one reason or another. Gasoline will quickly be used up and is not replaceable without our current infrastructure; the complexity of getting oil out of the ground, refining it, and transporting it will be all but impossible.

I next considered solar cells as a possible source of a limited amount of electricity. Then I discovered a book on "alternative energy" sources and changed my mind about not having energy available. With the right equipment and knowledge, the power company and gas station will not be missed that much.

Alternate energy sources include: wind, water, wood, methane, solar power, and probably others. These can be used for generating electricity, mechanical energy, chemical energy and heat, which can be converted to other forms of energy. As an example: electricity and chemical energy easily convert to heat or light.

To complement my background in electronics and support my interest in alternative energy sources, I am considering learning to be an electrician, not to the point of earning a living for the next few years, but at least enough so I can avoid some of the common mistakes in wiring for electricity. It is important to know what gauge of wire will support what amount of current, and how to protect circuits against overload and excessive heat that might start a fire. These are all areas of concern when wiring a house to support electricity generated by wind or solar power.

My interest in alternative energy has led me to consider learning welding. If you have sufficient power, you can weld. Or if you have the ability to collect, separate, and store the proper gases, you can weld. The ability to weld could be important in the survival environment.

These are just a few of the areas in which I am becoming interested and adding to my skill set. By the time this book is available, I hope to have added other skills.

You may want to consider adapting your current profession, area of expertise, or educational background as it would apply to this survival environment.

I recently read an informative article in *BackHome* magazine about making homemade soap.[1] This skill will be important in the future. From the article I learned that the main ingredients to homemade soap are lye and vegetable oil. Unfortunately, in the survival time you won't be able to run to the store and buy lye and vegetable oil. One of the more important skills needed is a "practical" chemist, an individual with a scientific or engineering background in chemistry who can work with the basics, someone who could make anything from concrete to medicines from the basic rocks, minerals, and other natural substances that will be the only materials available to use in the future. Or in my soap example, they could make lye and would know how to process vegetables to get vegetable oil.

---

[1]"Make Your Own Soap, Vegetarian Style," by Lynda McClanahan, *BackHome*, Fall 1992, page 39.

Another area important to the family or community will be medical skills. This covers the entire spectrum of medical personnel, including the surgeon, dentist, nurse, paramedic, chiropractor and massage therapist. The ideal person would be trained in one or more of these specialties, but know how to perform all of them. They too would need to go back to basics.

The purpose of this section is just to get you thinking. In Appendix 1, I have compiled a partial list of basic skills that will be important. I am sure there are many others. Some of these skills I strongly suggest you learn personally, such as growing food. Some skills may be available through others in your community (or commune) and can be bartered for, such as welding or mechanical skills.

There are a multitude of different places to obtain some of these basic skills, such as the local community college, trade schools and "Fun Ed" programs.

The materials and supplies you will need

As we go through this discussion you should think about two distinctly different time periods. These are **short term** and **long term**, and how they relate to the Preparation and Survival times. As an example, during the Preparation period, gasoline and electricity will still be available and relatively inexpensive. Thus a gas or electric chain saw will help you cultivate dead trees into usable fire wood. However the chain saw won't be much good during the Survival time if you don't have a continuing supply of gas or electricity.

A sealing machine will be useful during the Preparation time for sealing foods, seeds and even items such as tools to protect them from rusting. But this machine won't be useful during the Survival time, if you don't have electricity or you run out of the plastic sealing material. This is an example of an item that is helpful or necessary during the Preparation time only.

Food

First of all, you will need a certain amount of food to survive (short term) until you can grow your own (long term). How much will depend on your location and situation. If you move to a self-sufficient farm, your immediate or emergency food requirements may be minimal. But don't completely depend on the current crop, which could be wiped out by the storms, floods, tornados and other disasters that will happen during this period. I would say you will need a **bare minimum** supply of non-perishable foods to feed your family for at least two months.

The Mormons have been planning for this event or something like it for years. They suggest to their followers to have a **year's supply of essentials** (food, clothing, and, where possible, fuel). There can never be too much food under circumstances like this, but you have to be able to balance your ability to buy, and more significantly, store this much food. Keep in mind there will be other things you need to purchase and store. You might think these other items won't be important without enough food to survive, and I agree. But they may become very important when the stored food begins to run out, and when your survival goals become long term, instead of just the next meal, especially with items like farming tools, supplies, seeds, fertilizer, etc.

When I say that you will need enough to feed your family, you may discover you have a very large family, especially if you are known to be preparing for this event. Your favorite cousin, his wife, and six children may all of a sudden be there to "help" you through the crises. And of course, the cousin has also told the rest of the family that you have "plenty" and how to get to the farm. You may have been known as the family "kook" before all this started, and suddenly become the hero when it happens. The point being, you can't have too much food in storage. You can only have too little storage space and not enough money.

Producing food

The next area of concern should be getting in position to become self-sufficient and able to produce your own food—as soon as possible. The food might be produced in a hydroponics garden inside your home, in a garden, or on an entire farm. Again this depends on your particular situation, where you are located, and the money and other resources you have available to commit to this project.

This is an area you will have to start learning. Fortunately, there are plenty of books available to learn from.

Obviously you will need a supply of seeds for all the important crops you expect to grow. You will need tools and other equipment. Appendix 2 contains some suggested items.

Preparing food

You may be thinking that everything you eat during the critical times will be out of cans. If so, several hand can openers should definitely be on your list of required items. However, be prepared to cook food. You may want to have the tools and equipment to prepare and cook game for meat. With or without meat, you will need to be able to cook food, maybe even to bake items. To cook, you will need a supply of fuel. It might be something as simple as burning wood in an open pit or your home fireplace. If so, you will need a stockpile of wood and an adequate source of supply when this runs out. Or you might want to have a stove that burns gas, such as a camp stove. Consider both short-term and long-term requirements. A conventional camp stove may be adequate as long as you have the butane or appropriate fuel available. What do you do when the gas runs out? Is the stove convertible to other forms of fuel, such as wood? Probably not for most small camp stoves, but it might burn homemade methane, if you planned far enough ahead to develop a methane producing system. The camp stove might be the proper choice to throw into the trunk of the car before you leave town in a hurry.

If you planned and acted far enough ahead, you may already have installed a wood burning oven in your second residence, ready with a pile of dry wood on a farm with plenty of trees and sharp saws and axes.

Water supply

An emergency supply and continuing source of water is even more important than food. You can survive for a longer period of time without food than you can without water. So you need to store a supply of water for the short-term periods of emergencies and the three days of darkness. And you will need a long-term source of water to survive. This will affect your choice in selecting the site for your new residence. A flowing stream and well water are two sources of water. But open water will become contaminated, as might underground sources of water. So the ability to purify water is important to your survival. Water purification pills, household chlorine bleach (Clorox), and/or a water filtration system are necessary items.

The water filter (purification) system might be your most important piece of survival equipment. I recently read a book[2] that told of potential health-dangers to drinking today's tap water. These include: microorganisms, toxic minerals and metals, organic chemicals, radioactive substances and additives. Just imagine what the water quality will be like in an emergency or survival situation. Therefore, pick a good quality portable water filter as part of your survival equipment.

When you are planning on how much water to store for emergencies, consider that the average person needs approximately a gallon of water a day, and requires another gallon of

---

[2]*The Drinking Water Book: A Complete Guide to Safe Drinking Water* by Colin Ingram, 1991.

water for other things, such as cooking and washing. Thus the minimum amount of water that is needed, is two gallons of water per day, per person. For example, the amount of stored water for two people, for a week, would be twenty-eight gallons.

Physically and mentally preparing

The next few years, especially the time the earth turns, will cause much stress to the body. Getting in physical shape is necessary. If you move to the country and start working on the farm, it will provide many opportunities for natural exercise. However, until that time, you should start developing your body by whatever exercise capability you can justify. If you are like most of us, you need to add exercise into the master plan.

Start to think about living off the land. Plan family camping and fishing trips to get used to being outside and communing with nature.

Preparing for the three days of darkness

This is an exceptional time that must be prepared for separately. It is predicted that there will be three or more days of darkness at the time of the planet's turning. During the turning the Earth's gravitational field will be out of whack. The wave of energy that contributes to the polar shift may cause our electrical and electronic devices not to work for a while. If the predictions are accurate, something as simple as a flashlight might not work.

My suggestion is to prepare to handle several critical areas. One, you will need some form of **light**: to handle emergencies, instill comfort in yourself and others, disseminate meals, etc. I suggest you have flashlights handy, within easy reach. But they may not work during some or all of this period.

So I would also have a supply of candles, kerosene lamps, and/or chemical "break lights." I suggest the chemical lights be used as the main source of light. They don't consume the oxygen in the room or contain any form of a flame that might start a fire. Candles, when used, should be in containers that block the wind from blowing them out. Obviously candles and kerosene lamps require that you have matches or other means of lighting them. Flashlights require good batteries.

Secondly, select a safe area and seal off this room or area you plan on using during this period. This means seal windows and cracks beneath doors so the contaminated air will not enter the room. However, you must provide some source of clean or filtered air. The last thing you want to do is have a completely sealed room and have everyone die of asphyxiation while sleeping, as might occur if you are using candles or kerosene lamps that use up the oxygen in the room. To seal off the room and yet provide air will mean providing some area(s) that has access to the outside air with filters installed. An ideal place to install a filtered air inlet would be where there is a good supply of unfiltered air available, but where this space is protected from the outside of the building. Thus the filter might be installed in the floor where the house or shelter has a basement, or in the wall to other rooms that have air flowing through them. This would mean that you need to leave windows open in this outside room. These air vents should have covers available to seal them during the worst part of the crises, but remove them to get the filtered air when needed.

It would be prudent to have a secondary supply of air, such as having compressed air[3] stored in diver's tanks. These tanks usually hold only an hour or so of air for divers underwater, but might be appropriate for a supplemental air supply if breathing gets difficult at times. A diver's "regulator" would allow you to breathe the air from the tanks without waste.

---

[3]Beware using compressed oxygen. This could be dangerous, especially if candles are being used in the room.

If you must go outside for emergency reasons, or your sealed area is breached, you will need some breathing devices, something similar to a gas mask. The masks used by painters might be adequate. And I suggest that you have a stock of the inexpensive dust masks as a minimum.

The third area of preparation is for food and water. Three (or more) days is too long to go without food and water. Food and water should already be part of your overall planning. But due to the unusual circumstances at this time—you will need to have water and ready-to-eat food in your survival room.

The fourth area of preparation concerns the problem of gravity. People could be forced to the floor during this time, and the only way to move about will be limited to moving on their bellies. We could experience something similar to the acceleration that astronauts and jet pilots experience. I don't know if this is accurate, or if it is, how widespread this problem will be. What I suggest in this case is to have chemical break lights and a supply of emergency food and water near the floor of your protected area.

This gravity problem is probably the most far-out of any of the predictions I've received, but it keeps occurring, so I'm passing it along. I feel it is better to look stupid and be prepared, than to have it happen and not be prepared. One way you look stupid. The other way, you might be dead. Put in this perspective—looking stupid is not so bad! Besides, you are in good company. I suspect Noah had the same problem. You know who got the last laugh in Noah's day!

Summary

I could go on and on about what skills, materials and supplies we should have, but most of this is up to you, depending on how serious you are about preparing, and how much time and money you commit to this effort. The important thing is that you think through this process, plan ahead, then act on your plan.

Appendices 2 and 3 list items that might be required, both important and optional items.

CHAPTER

4

Preparing for Natural Disasters

PREPARING FOR NATURAL DISASTERS IS IMPORTANT, whether or not you believe in the predictions. There is some overlapping of information between this chapter and others, due to the nature of being prepared for emergencies in general.

The earthquakes have already started in California, volcanoes have occurred in the Philippines and Japan, and a huge storm killed over 100,000 people in Bangladesh at the end of April in 1991. In Texas, we have the Gulf coast that has hurricanes and the northern part of Texas is in "tornado alley." Even while this guide was being written,[1] Hurricane Andrew had just lashed Florida and Louisiana, taking lives and doing a considerable amount of damage. Andrew was described as one of the largest storms ever, with wind gusts reaching as high as 200 miles per hour.[2] The following week a huge tidal wave

---

[1]Hurricane Andrew reached Florida on August 24 and Louisiana on the 26th, 1992.
[2]Gordon-Michael Scallion in "The Earth Changes Report" Issue No. 11, July 25, 1992, pages 3 and 4, predicted that Florida would experience two hurricanes. The first one would "be the largest recorded in Florida's history, with winds, at times, exceeding 150 miles per hour. This (first) one is to occur between August 15th and Sept. 27th, 1992." Then Hurricane Andrew happened in August, 1992.

struck Nicaragua, there was an earthquake in southern Utah, and a killer storm struck China.

Mother Mary has told us that the storms will continue to grow in size and frequency, and that no area will be immune to its share of problems. It has also been mentioned that no one knows where the old fault lines are, so earthquakes and volcanoes could happen in places that have never experienced these before. So far, most areas of the United States have been fortunate enough to miss a really major disaster, but this is going to change. Even the skeptical should appreciate the need for emergency preparation.

What can we do? Similar to our long range planning for the polar shift, we need a plan. We need to be prepared for any emergency. This will include having an emergency kit, food and water, ready to go on a moment's notice. First-aid training and an adequate first-aid kit are essential. Families with children should develop and practice fire, earthquake and tornado drills. Do you know the safest spot in your house to take cover from an approaching tornado? What if you are in a car? Should you stay inside a building or go outside for an earthquake? What do you do if you are caught outside during a severe lightning storm? Do you know where the closest local emergency shelter is located or how to get to it? These are just some of the issues that need to be covered in an emergency preparedness plan.

The idea behind schools having regular fire drills (and other emergency drills) is to prepare the children so they won't be afraid. A family plan should involve everyone in the family. Everyone should have an assigned task. If there is an elderly person, one of the older children should be assigned to get that person to safety or into the car. Another should be assigned to get the emergency kit, another the food and water. Basically everyone should be involved in the emergency plan. The plan should be practiced in the form of an **emergency drill**. A map or diagram could be used showing the rooms of the home and to whom each responsibility is assigned. The diagram would show the location of the emergency supplies and to whom a particular responsibility is assigned. The training should employ as many senses as possible. You need to see it, hear it, feel it, do it—so that it will become an automatic reflex.

A family plan should cover contingencies, like what to do if the children are separated from their parents when an emergency happens. If they are close to home, should they meet at their house? Or stay at the school or at a friend's home. If the children find themselves at home by themselves, they should know where the emergency food and water are kept. They should be instructed in emergency procedures, such as turning on a portable radio to find out about weather conditions. Children that are old enough should be taught basic first aid. Scouting programs are a good method for training these young people. Older children should be taught how to take care of the younger children. How they should "take control" and keep the younger children busy playing games or singing, if the parents are away or busy handling the different aspects of the emergency. All this is a part of the emergency plan.

First Aid Training

When the disasters start happening, emergency medical services will be overloaded. You won't be able to call the fire department and have an ambulance with paramedics arrive. You must become **self-reliant**. The first thing you could do is take a formal first aid course. The American Red Cross offers such a course. In our area they are taught every Monday, Wednesday and Saturday. The cost is $30.00 for an eight-hour session that includes CPR. To register, call at least three days in advance. Consult your local telephone book for the phone number of the nearest American Red Cross location.

Consider that first aid and lifesaving skills may be needed to save the life of a neighbor, stranger, or even your loved ones. Or if the situation is reversed, anyone of these might be able to save your life. Therefore, you will want everyone you know to have these skills.

The Essentials (Food, Water, Light/Heat)

A supply of food and water is essential to your survival. Again, if a major disaster occurs, supplies of food and water will be interrupted. As an example of what can and will happen, the news broadcast after Hurricane Andrew (Aug., 1992) showed people standing in long lines waiting on the "government" to supply food and water. In a disaster, water supplies can be contaminated and/or pumping stations destroyed. Food, even if temporarily available, will be sold out in a short time, as people make "runs" on stores.

Water is more important than food. You can survive longer without food than you can without water. So start saving water in extra containers. The most obvious is your camping gear thermos jug. Fill it and put it back in storage with water in it. Save plastic soft drink containers filled with tap water and store them in your garage or closets. You may want to purchase some spring or distilled water from the grocery store. You should also have some water purification tablets and a bottle of household chlorine bleach (Clorox)[3] handy.

When an emergency happens, start emergency procedures immediately. If you are at home, fill your bath tubs with water, while there is still water pressure. Consider other sources of fresh stored water, such as your water heater and commode tanks. Don't flush the commode until you've saved the supply of clean water. You can then fill the commode tanks with water that is not suitable for drinking or cleaning. Such as water from a nearby pond, swimming pool or hot tub. The commodes are not electrical and do not require water pressure to flush.

---

[3]Clorox can be used to purify water by adding a few drops to a gallon of water.

Build up a supply of food for emergencies, food that can be prepared without cooking. Be aware of the shelf life of the food supply. Rotate it by eating it before it becomes outdated and replacing it with freshly purchased units. Your emergency food supply should be ready to be moved on short notice. If you have to vacate your home in a hurry, you will need to have boxes or containers ready to go. These containers might be heavy duty cloth containers or rigid plastic "tool box" type units, preferably something with handles.

One kind of food designed for emergencies is the military MREs (Meals-Ready-to-Eat). These meals have been designed to be flavorful, and last five to nine years without refrigeration. A full meal MRE contains an entree, supplementary dish, a dessert, and an accessory pack that contains drinks, salt and pepper, and a spoon. They are fully cooked, so they can be eaten cold, or warmed by a number of methods. These can be found at Army Navy supply stores and some mail order companies.

Another variety of food that is available for emergency situations is freeze-dried and dehydrated foods. One particular vendor offers a "no-cook" type of food that requires only water to reconstitute. Just add water and eat. This supplier has food in foil pouches for events like camping trips, and in #10 and #2½ can sizes for storage and large scale feedings. These are available through sporting-good stores, survival stores, or mail order.

If the emergency is such that you are able to remain at home, but the electricity goes out, here are a few things to consider. You will need a source of light and heat available. Light can be a great comfort in darkness, and heat is necessary during cold seasons and for cooking food. Light can be provided by flashlights, candles, kerosene lamps and chemical break lights.

Sources of heat and cooking fires includes wood and gas. If you have a butane or propane cooker and extra fuel, you may be in pretty good shape. You may want to get an extra tank or two for your cooker and keep it filled. Depending on the seriousness of the emergency, you might want to bring the cooker inside your secure area. Don't just leave it in the back yard to be taken by someone that thinks they need it more than you do. However, be aware that charcoal gives off dangerous fumes and any fire uses up the oxygen in a room. So, keep a window open to supply fresh air as long as the fire is going. Likewise, if you have firewood outside, bring it inside. During prolonged times of emergency, others may want to take things from you. Don't make it too easy.

If an emergency happens during the warm season, you will need to consider the preservation of food in your freezer. If the ambient temperature is not too warm, the food in your freezer may last several days or so. Keep the freezer door closed, maybe even tape it closed, so no one "forgets." When you do open it, prepare or eat what is available before it goes bad. Save canned goods until after the frozen foods are gone.

The Emergency Kit

Develop an emergency kit containing essential items. The most important part of an emergency kit is a first aid kit or the equivalent. Besides the normal bandages, this kit should include over-the-counter medicines and remedies (tylenol, cough syrup, hydrocortisone ointment, etc). The kit should contain survival (camping) items like a flashlight, can openers, cooking utensils, matches, transistor radio, water purification tablets, rope, compass, shovel, axe/hatchet, knives, etc. Personal items to include: toilet paper, tooth brush, soap, rain coat, gloves, etc. And there will be items that are associated with the emergency kit, but too large to fit inside a container, for example a tent, camp stools, cots, etc.

Appendix 3, Emergency Supplies, has a list of other items considered important for the kit. However you should personalize it for your family. This kit should be in one (or more) container with handles for easy portability. If you are able to remain in your home during the emergency, it provides you with a central place to organize and contain the emergency items. If you must leave home quickly, you can grab the emergency kit, food, water and personal items (clothes, medicines, etc.) and put them into your car.

Summary

To review, you need an emergency plan. You need to become proficient in first aid and lifesaving techniques. You need an emergency kit, and supply of food and water, that can be loaded into your car in a matter of minutes. The emergency supplies should be in a central place known to everyone. Keep your car in good running shape, so you can respond to emergencies; especially keep it at least half full of gas. Practice your emergency drills! And most of all, keep a clear head and try not to panic when a real emergency exists.

Other sources of information

After working on this chapter and while researching other sources of information, I came across a three-volume set called the *Family Emergency Plan* by Barry and Lynette Crockett. This is an excellent set of manuals that covers, in specific detail, how to prepare for all kinds of natural disasters and emergencies, where I've only been able to touch on some of these issues.

Volume 1 includes having a family emergency and evacuation plan, teaching children about emergencies, 72-hour emergency kits, earthquake/winter storm car kits, first aid kits, finding safe water in an emergency and much more. Volume 2 covers how to prepare for: earthquakes, tsunami (tidal wave), volcanic ashfall, landslides and mudslides, avalanches, dam failures, structural fires, and more. Volume 3 covers: hurricanes, tornados, lightning and severe thunderstorms, flash floods, river floods, winter storms, drought and extreme heat, forest fires and wildfires, nuclear attack and radiological accidents, and developing national emergency.

The *Family Emergency Plan* volumes are very detailed with information. Volume 3, for example, has ten pages devoted to hurricanes and explains the difference between a hurricane watch and a hurricane warning. Then it covers what to do at the beginning of the hurricane season, before the hurricane, during the hurricane, what to do at the shelter, and after the "all-clear" is given.

Your local Civil Defense Office of Emergency Preparedness is another good source of information and literature. I called the Dallas office and was sent information on: emergency preparedness checklist, floods, tornados, fires and severe weather. They didn't have any information on earthquakes, so I had a friend in California contact his local Office of Emergency Services. He forwarded "Beat the Quake!" information to me. These included "Plans to Make" and "Steps to Take" that covered emergency supplies checklist and items to store.

5

Suggestions for Accumulating Materials and Supplies

THE LIST OF "MATERIALS AND SUPPLIES" in Appendix 2 is fairly long. To run out and purchase a major portion of these would be a heavy investment. All of us have limited resources when it comes to time and money. If we have more time than money, we can use some of the time to save money in acquiring a few of these items.

Here are some ideas that we have had and are using to start collecting and/or stockpiling these items.

Garage Sales

One of the best sources for inexpensive items is garage sales. A popular garage sale item that we started stocking up on is candles. I've bought large, often new candles for as low as 10 cents each. To work the garage sales takes a fair amount of time, usually on weekends. The trade off is that you can get some great bargains on items that you just couldn't afford or justify purchasing. Garage sales are a likely source of items such as: fishing equipment, used hand tools, bicycles, bows and arrows, sealing machines, "how-to" books, and the more common items like clothes.

In my reading I came across "Pamela's Pennypincher"[1] newsletter. The March 1992 issue had an article "Garage Sales: My Favorite Pastime." This taught me the value in "bargaining" at garage sales. Pamela writes, "Bargaining is the name of the game at garage sales whether you are on the buy side, or the sell side." I immediately tried it the next weekend and it worked. Several times I offered only half of what they were asking and bought it. Pamela suggested that they want to get rid of these items, that is why they are there. One prize that I purchased for $1.50, was a clean, current book on gardening, worth $24.95, and which I had considered buying at a local bookstore. Thus bargaining stretches out your limited resources to allow you to buy more items.

Pawn Shops

These may be a source for items like tools, welding equipment and a number of unusual items. You will likely pay more for the same item than if you found it in a garage sale.

Wholesale Clubs/Warehouse Stores
(example: Sam's, Pace, Price Club, etc.)

Here is where you can find large quantities of some of the food stuffs at reasonable prices. Some of the items we will probably purchase here, are large sacks of rice and beans. The timing of getting this type food is somewhat important. You

---

[1]"Pamela's Pennypincher," 39 Green Meadow Blvd., Middletown, NJ 07748. $12.00 for 12 monthly issues.

can't wait to the last minute to get them, but you don't want to buy them too soon, unless you have plenty of storage area already available. And if you do buy early, be sure and find some method of packaging. Rats and insects can get at stored staples. We are thinking of large metal cans in which we can seal entire sacks of food.

Mail Order Sources

Some items are just not readily available at local stores. The alternative energy products and equipment are examples. There are stores and dealers in some parts of the country, but there is an apparent lack of them around Texas, probably because Texas has for ages had cheap energy and good access to the electrical grid.

Probably the best sources of information I have found on these subjects are the magazines,[2] *Home Power*, *BackHome*, and *Backwoods Home Magazine*. Their articles cover survival type information, such as: solar cooking, a primer on welding, living off the grid, and many others. The magazines are full of ads for mail order suppliers of alternative energy, gardening, and survival products. Many of these charge $1 to $3 for catalogs, and most will credit this against a purchase.

Food that is specially packaged for long shelf life is also available from mail order companies. This is typically low-moisture, nitrogen-packed food that is just not available at your local grocer.

I've also found that the Sears catalog has quite a few items that might be needed. Some of these include items like gasoline generators, wood stoves, water distillers, and submersible water pumps.

---

[2]See Appendix 4 for contact information.

Army and Navy Stores

These are a good source for some of the more unique camping and outdoor equipment. Examples are water purification pills and the chemical break lights I've mentioned.

Other Ideas

Bartering is something I have not yet tried, but might work well for some people. The bartering I am referring to is similar to what will be required during the survival time. However, today's bartering is a little different. There are "bartering associations" that act as brokers and deal in barter credits.

"Swap-Fests" and "Flea Markets" are similar to garage sales. In some cases you may be able to trade items (barter) instead of using up cash for the purchase. In "Pamela's Pennypincher" newsletter she mentioned that a future issue will feature "Bartering is in."

Auctions are another potential source. Items like tools and welding equipment are quite common at auctions. Sometimes at auctions you can get bargains. But often people bidding go crazy and pay as much as retail or even more. You just never know what will happen at an auction. An auction may take a full day (or more) to buy a few items. So you have to trade off the value of your time versus the potential savings. But auctions can be fun; consider the time invested as "entertainment" time. Just a word of warning. Many auction companies won't take a personal check. Check their rules about payment in advance.

The local newspaper "Classified Ads" section is a good source for spotting garage sales, swap fests, auctions, and for particular items you may want to acquire.

6

Selecting Your Survival Home

IT SOUNDS LIKE THIS CHAPTER should be the blueprint for designing a bomb or storm shelter. What I am really suggesting are things to consider when picking a "back-to-the-land" home. These are suggestions of the way I perceive it should be done.

Practical Survival magazine had a couple of good articles in the June/July 1992 issue titled, "Getting Out" and subtitled "Relocating With Survival in Mind" by Steve Miller and "Making Your Own Great Escape" by Al Doyle. These had several good suggestions. The main theme is to plan your move. Make lists of what you are wanting or require in selecting a new area. Contact the chambers of commerce for potential locations and subscribe to local newspapers to see what is going on in an area.

BackHome magazine[1] had an article "Sizing Up a Country House" by Alan Schabilion, that discussed what to look for when you buy a country home. It discussed how to check the plumbing, wiring, walls, floors, kitchens, attics and generally

---

[1]*BackHome* magazine, Summer 1992, pages 29-31 (see References for obtaining).

what to look for to make sure you know what you are getting for your money. Alan is the author of *Country Dreams, Your Guide to Saving Time and Money While Still Getting What You Want and Need in Country Property!*

I'll share with you how I envision my "back-to-the-land" home. The requirements include:

1. Preferably a wooded area, but with enough open spaces where solar devices and a greenhouse can have access to the sun's rays throughout the entire day, and where a wind generator can get adequate wind without being blocked by trees or hills, eliminating the need to be so high above ground.

2. The area should be adequate for farming, with an area fairly near the house for a garden. An existing greenhouse would be a nice addition.

3. The region should have good sunlight all year round and good prevailing winds to drive a wind generator.

4. It should be within about one or two hour's drive of a major airport, and within twenty minutes from some medical facility, such as a hospital.

5. It should have a well for fresh water, preferably with a stream going through the property, which would be a source of water and be able to support some form of hydro power. This could be a water wheel for mechanical or electrical energy.

6. The house would have both a basement and an attic. The basement could be a storm shelter.

7. There needs to be a barn or some other building for storage (this might be built later).

8. There should be no deed restrictions on the property to limit: antennas, damming the stream, or any kind of construction in general.

9. The property would have adequate access to it from the existing roadways.

10. The state should have low or no income tax. And state and local laws should not prohibit guns, survival tools and alternative energy equipment.

7

Communities

I N THE FUTURE, THE COMMUNITY will replace the urban environment that most of us reside in. The community will be composed of like-minded people joined together for the common good.

It seems that every spiritually-oriented psychic I talk with is being guided to start a "community"—to leave the city and go to a rural or farm area. Several are acquaintances and would naturally join together, but their guides are telling them to start their own community.

In June 1992 (and again in September), Annie and I visited one such community, Sparrow Hawk Village, in the northeastern corner of Oklahoma. This is an intentional, spiritually-oriented, community. It is built on a mountain in the western end of the Ozark mountains near Tahlequah, Oklahoma, about 65 miles southeast of Tulsa.

Sparrow Hawk Village was founded in 1981 by Reverend Carol Parrish-Harra and her husband, Charles Harra. They have forty privately owned homes and eighty full-time residents (as of June 1992), and yes, they do have electricity and indoor plumbing.

Carol is the spiritual leader and founder of the "Light of Christ Community Church" and Charles is the planning genius of the village.

During our first visit, Charles spent most of a day showing us the community and the energy-efficient homes he designed. Sparrow Hawk Village has its own volunteer fire department, church, new age book store, gift shop, library, greenhouse, water supply and backup emergency generator. The church has a basement that is designed as an emergency shelter with a #2 earthquake rating and would withstand nuclear fallout.

The 400 acres is divided into thirds. One third is for private homes and community buildings, one third for agriculture purposes, and the last third is to remain as a natural wooded habitat.

The community has a heavy spiritual emphasis, and everyone is extremely friendly and helpful.

They have a democratic form of government. Committees handle different responsibilities. A couple of these are the agriculture and emergency planning committees.

Sparrow Hawk Village held their first "Discover Community—Its Virtues and Its Challenges" workshop over the Labor Day Weekend, September 4 to 7, 1992. The workshop was designed for those wanting to join a community, create a community, or successfully maintain an existing community. They discussed their personal experiences, hopes and disappointments, as well as a complete discussion of their ten-year history of building a community from the ground up (no roads! no water!). The guests shared their hopes and expectations with each other and the Village staff. This first workshop was so successful that they will offer it every Labor Day.

To quote from their Sancta Sophia Seminary catalog, " A visit to a spiritual community such as Sparrow Hawk Village is a unique experience of de-light! A new lifestyle emphasizing love, beauty, freedom and joy is waiting to be experienced."

I can give personal witness that this is a wonderful place to visit and for some a wonderful place to live.

Another source of information regarding communities was found in a newsletter titled, "Rocky Mountain CoHousing Quarterly." In "An Introduction to CoHousing,"

> CoHousing communities are resident-developed cooperative neighborhoods where individual households are clustered around a common house with shared facilities such as a dining room, an area for child care, workshops and laundry. Each home is self sufficient with a complete kitchen, but dinners are often available in the common house for those who wish to participate.
>
> These developments are also unique in that they are organized, planned and managed by the residents themselves. By re-defining the neighborhood concept to better address contemporary lifestyles, CoHousing communities can create cross-generational communities for singles, families and the elderly.
>
> CoHousing was "born" in Denmark almost 20 years ago out of a desire to create cooperative housing that satisfied the needs of changing lifestyles. CoHousing developments in Europe, range in size from six to eighty households, with the majority between 15 to 33.
>
> This form of community development was brought to the United States in 1988 by Kathryn McCamant and Charles Durrett, a husband-wife design team based in Berkeley, California. Here in the United States over 100 groups are in various stages of development. According to McCamant and Durrett these projects are based on democratic principles that espouse no ideology other than the desire for a more practical and social home environment.

The community I envision will have to become self-sustainable in as short a time as possible. They will have to prepare for their common welfare, defense and law and order, grow food, teach the young, provide medical care, and be able to live together as a functioning unit.

Living together as a functioning unit isn't easy. Beforehand, individuals need to clear away emotional pain, hurts, obsessions and addictions. We address this in the chapter on

"The Spiritual Connection." Annie sees a need for support groups—perhaps male/female groups, inter-generational support groups, and children support groups which address how individuals are feeling. A support group allows for the open and honest venting of feelings without criticism. They could be set up along the lines of a "12-Step" program, which allows each person to speak about their feelings, remembering that feelings are real to the person, and feelings need to aired. We see an emphasis on prayer and meditation, allowing and honoring each person's individuality and uniqueness.

The American way of being individual and being "right" will have to be put aside in order to live peacefully. The emphasis will be on what's good for the whole. What does this community need and what's best for the community. We will need to start changing how we view ourselves, our family and the community we are now living in. By changing our attitude of what's important for "me" to what's important to "us," we begin to set up an aura of peace within our group. I like the song whose first line is, "Let there be peace on earth and let it begin with me." It says a lot about how we need to prepare for living in a community like this.

Rules and regulations are needed, but so is understanding and compassion. One is not more important than the other. It all needs to be an integral part of life in a community.

One other method of forming a community could be patterned after the Amish. They each live on their own land, but during certain times they come together for the good of the community. We could help each other with planting, harvesting, canning and curing of foods, and with alternative energy.

Many of us will need to learn so many new skills that it seems almost an impossibility. One advantage I see in a community is that many people will already be semi-knowledgeable in many of the important skills. The young and strong of body are needed, but so are the older, more experienced persons. By pooling talents and skills we can have a fairly comfortable life in trying times. Everyone will have a place and a function; it's the only way a community geared for survival can work.

Before a person ever becomes a part of or starts a community, they need to ask themselves some questions. What do I expect from a community? What do I have to offer a community? What can I live with? What do I need as a person to be happy? What can I tolerate? What are the things which I simply cannot live with? Am I willing to be part of a group? Can I allow others to be themselves without any judgments? Do I know my limits? Basically can I take care of myself? Can I be responsible for my actions? Do I know how to express my feelings? Can I say "this bothers me" without becoming upset or angry? How much privacy do I require? How much space do I need in order to feel comfortable? What is my purpose in seeking a community?

In the beginning we all tend to look at community as an idyllic way of life. But we are humans, and each of us will enter a community with our own set of problems, unresolved issues, judgments and expectations. All these things make us unique and individual. In order to live in a community we need to take the rose-colored glasses off and look at how we interact with our family. This is how we will interact with others who are living in the closeness of a community.

There needs to be a time period of soul searching. One must find what he/she expects from a community. Do you expect to be taken care of? Then ask yourself this question: Do I want to take care of others? What if everyone expects to be taken care of? We are not alone in our quest nor in our motives. Do I expect to be loved and have all my emotional needs fulfilled? If you find a twinge within suggesting a yes, you need to do some inner work. No one can fulfill all your emotional needs. Take a good look and see what unresolved issues you need to clear away first. You can't expect a community to do your inner work or fulfill your needs.

Do an inventory of your talents, skills, hobbies and interests. These are the things you have to offer a community. Leave out nothing. Can I cook, sew, play an instrument? Cooking and sewing are very important, but so is music and entertainment. Can you fish, plant a garden, frame a building, wire electrical circuits, repair tools, etc.? When you know what you have to offer, then you can locate a community which will have need of you and in which you will be able to express yourself. Find a community which is well rounded. If you like music and become a part of community of musicians, you may have your need for music covered, but how about food or water? Be realistic about yourself and the community you're considering.

What each of us needs to be a happy person is a tough question. Think and list all the things you now need, understanding that needs change according to circumstances. As an example, if you live in a city, your needs will be met by a balance of city life and privacy. You need time to enjoy friends, family, and your way of life. But if you are living as part of a close knit community, your needs will be met in many different ways. Consider some basic things you need to be happy, such as food. This is a very important issue when living in a group environment with communal meals. Some communities may be vegetarian, and if you like meat, you will not be happy in such a community. On the other hand, if you are a vegetarian and you live with a bunch of meat eaters, you won't be happy either. Do you enjoy a lot of time alone? Then you will need to include this as a must when you look into a community. Remembering that there will be rules and regulations, also there is always peer pressure.

What can I live with? What can I tolerate? Make a list of attitudes, beliefs and personality traits which will be uncomfortable to you. Each community has a personality of its own. Annie is very uncomfortable around guns, so this would be one thing she would have a hard time tolerating. Is there a lot of fear? Or is there peace in relying on a Higher Power? What practices simply set your hair on end? These will be the things which you cannot tolerate. So take a good look at your likes and dislikes. Take a good look at the likes and dislikes of the leaders of a community.

One very important trait to look at in yourself is the ability to take care of yourself emotionally, as well as physically. Can you set limits and boundaries? This may not seem like a big deal now, but when confronted with people who are imposing on your person, time, energy or talents, you will need to know how to care for yourself. If this is a problem, I would suggest you start to work on it immediately. Everyone needs to know how to care for their person, their emotions and their needs.

Visit different communities whether you plan to start one or join one. Check out their style, government and what they believe in. Is there a respect for both men and women? If the community leans toward one in favor of the other, it is off balance, and this will lead to problems. Are you comfortable with the way men and women are treated? By all means look closely at the leader or leaders. Are they respectful of everyone? Do they practice what they espouse? Can the leaders make decisions without conflict? Is there an air of togetherness or separation? How do they govern themselves? Is it by consensus or vote? Does everyone participate and join in? How will you provide a living for yourself and your loved ones? What does the outside community think about the inner community? Visit the towns nearby and talk to people and ask about the community. What's their reputation? If you join this community, this will be your reputation too.

When a person has done this much soul searching, they know themselves and what they are looking for in life and in a community. It may seem like too much work, but without this up-front inner work, there is a tendency to jump first and think later.

I feel one of the most important aspects of community is what goes on spiritually—how the spiritual aspect of the community is dealt with, acted out and lived daily. Here again you must be clear about your definition of spiritual needs, what one perceives as important and necessary in their lives for their spiritual needs to be met. One must be in agreement with the community's basic philosophy and with their spiritual philosophy.

Just as our society has grown away from the larger, extended families of olden times, the future will bring a return to communities, so take the time to consider yourself, your family and your potential role in a community.

8

The Spiritual Connection

T HE INTENT OF THIS "SURVIVAL GUIDE" is to motivate you to prepare physically to survive the coming Earth changes. However, I don't want to overemphasize the importance of this over the need to be *spiritually* prepared. It would be very easy to get lost in material concerns and ignore the important inner work that needs to be done.

In the course of working with Annie on *Mary's Message* and the following work that she is doing, we have learned that our earthly existence is but a practice session for our real life in the Spirit World. What we do on earth helps us progress (or digress) in our life goals, but this is not our "real" life. Our real life is the eternal life that exists in Spirit.

I am not advocating any particular religion or belief system. However, I encourage you to spend time daily in meditation and prayer, and make the connection to the Father within. That connection will guide and help you through these trying times. The physical preparation will ultimately be a waste of time if you are not prepared spiritually.

From Jesus' message in *Mary's Message,*

Know that the answer to your survival is in your mind and heart. It is through the kingdom of God that you will receive your answers. See, when faced with the possibilities of these disasters, where are your money, clothes, cars, houses and job? Where is all you have placed value in? How will your money or your profession help you? How will having the right clothes and the best house be of benefit to you? Where will your job get you? How will your education help?

These are things of this world. They are of this world and for this world. In the long run they will not help you with your true life.[1]

Why address the subject of spirituality in a practical manual? Because to have a strong belief in a loving Creator, a benevolent God, gives one a sense of constancy. It connects us to our innate common sense. What mankind calls common sense is in reality our connection to Universal Wisdom, and this connection is essential for our self-confidence, self-reliance, and an attitude of can-do. **To be wise is to be prepared**.

Through a daily regimen of prayer and meditation we make our connection to the place of wisdom which is within our hearts. From the new information which Mary is giving, Her whole emphasis is on **inner guidance**. For those of us who are more down to earth, we can call it gut instinct, common sense or inner-knowing. The key to getting in touch with our own inner guidance is to ask questions, get quiet, still our thoughts and feelings, and listen. It isn't easy. The answer can enter our mind at the most unusual time. It may be a feeling or gut reaction, or perhaps a click that is set off within our body. You just *know* that you know. This inner knowingness is what will be needed in order to remain calm and balanced.

It is very important to trust yourself and your inner guidance. If you have been prudent and learned all you can about personal survival, this will give self-confidence. The people who can keep their wits about them will have the easiest time.

---

[1]MM, chapter 10, pages 177-178

The spiritual connection is a very practical connection to your inner self, to the common sense which is innate in everyone. The spiritual connection opens you up to gut feelings about situations and will help you avoid panic. Panic is a natural reaction during a crisis; it shuts down the mind with an over-load of fear. Then you cannot think or feel your inner guidance. The spiritual connection gives one a whole different point of view and allows us to act wisely in critical situations. We view the events from a calmer, self-assured perspective. It's the inner assurance that you can think, act and find a solution to any problem.

By being spiritually connected, you will find new strengths, a determination to find solutions, and the ability to be "present" during a crisis and aware of all that is happening around you. By being present, you are aware of your surround-ings, the circumstance or crisis, and the immediate need. You not only know what to do, but how to do it—how to improvise if there is a shortage of supplies; what to use to improvise and how to make supplies last; how to direct people to help them-selves and others. In a panic, the mind is put on hold, while you either flee or fight. This could cause harm to yourself and the people you are responsible for. **The spiritual connection is essential!** When you can rely and trust yourself to hear within, you will be able to really help. You will lead others to remain as calm as possible under the circumstances. Many will be saved from more pain or harm by remaining calm.

Panic can cause you to give away your personal power. Why give your power away to someone else? Just think about the Jonesboro tragedy which happened a few years ago in Guyana. The people who followed Jones into the jungle were afraid and gave him all their power. They allowed one man to make all their decisions, because they thought he had a strong spiritual connection. When he ordered everyone to drink the poison, and some didn't want to, they were shot. Most drank the poison and died. Sad, but that's what can happen when you are not spiritually connected. If you are living in fear, it's so easy to be lulled into thinking that you have found someone to take all your problems away. A spiritually strong person will not need another person to think for him or her.

How do you connect spiritually? It's different for everyone. What works for me may not work for you. Mother Mary says that our true spiritual connection comes through prayer and meditation; prayer is talking to God and meditation is listening. Sound easy? Let me attest to the fact it takes work, persistence and perseverance. That's why it's necessary to begin now. Now, this minute, begin to follow what your inner guidance is finding to be true for you. This is how to connect to Universal Wisdom. There is no need to justify yourself to others; simply say, "I think" or "I feel this is wise." After all, it is *you* thinking as you should, with your full mind. To think while spiritually connected allows an expansion to take place within your mind to new areas of information. We don't need to know *how* the mind works, just accept the fact that **you can trust your inner guidance.** Accept this with confidence, and you will be prepared for any event which may enter your life.

Who are we preparing for? For ourselves, our loved ones, friends, neighbors and anyone who is there. I've been asked, what if you don't survive, why prepare for others? Because we all have a vested interest in humanity surviving, and we can best help others if we are spiritually strong.

Our true spiritual connection goes beyond religion or dogma to the "Innate Essence" of mankind. Practice your religion, do all the things which make you feel connected to your idea of a Higher Power. Call Him/Her God, Higher Power, Allah or Great Spirit. But connect to that Essence within that is truly beyond explanation or expression.

People who are spiritual radiate strength, not just physical strength, but a strength of conviction, an ability to see truth in every situation. They can quickly assess a situation and decide what needs to be done and how to do it. These people may or may not even be aware of their spiritual strength. They may believe in their own abilities or in a Higher Power. Whatever it is, their spiritual connection gives them the self-confidence and ability to act correctly or appropriately.

Not only do the spiritually connected have inner strength, but they also have an ability to lead with gentleness. They can be a follower or a leader, because the nature of a spiritually connected person is to work for the good of the majority. As more and more people connect to their own inner Source of Wisdom, the hope of our future is assured. In times of stress, we all need a good measure of gentleness and tenderness. It soothes the heart and the soul. In a gentle and appropriate way spiritually connected people can heal the wounds of trauma because they have the ability to give love unconditionally.

The spiritual connection will aid you in facing your fears, especially the grand-daddy of all fears, the fear of death. It helps us face the unknown and make peace with our own immortality. Then we can really begin to prepare for all events with wisdom, peace, and hope for the future.

To prepare for physical and spiritual survival, we need to learn and grow, and use *all* of our resources. Our earnest seeking and our sincerity count the most. We have been told that God made us all individual and uniquely different, and that's the way He relates to us, individually and uniquely. It's wonderful that our own guru is inside us. He is there in our minds and hearts waiting for our call.

1

Skills

Level I--everyone should have a basic knowledge of these.

1. Farming and growing food
2. First aid
3. Teaching—enough to pass your area of expertise to the next generation

Level II--optional skills that you should have.

1. Water purification--to provide safe drinking water
2. Hunting--how to hunt and prepare the kill
3. Animal husbandry--how to feed and care for animals
4. Making soap, rope, glue, etc--basic stuff
5. Herbal remedies

Level III--skills required by at least one person in the family, commune, or community.

1. Medical--doctor, nurse, EMT (emergency medical technician), dentists, chiropractors, opticians, massage therapists, etc.
2. Welding
3. Chemist--for medicines, water analyzing, working with oil and gases, making concrete, developing animal feeds
4. Construction--home building, repairing, etc.
5. Mechanical--general, maybe with a background in automobiles, air conditioning, plumbing, etc.
6. Electrician
7. Electronics and computers--especially alternative energy sources.
8. Teachers--for basic and specialized education.
9. Glass making
10. Metal making and working
11. Lumber processing and wood working

2

Materials and Supplies
(For all phases: short term, long term)

Food and related items:

> Enough non-perishable food for your family's needs for a minimum of two months and preferably up to a one year supply.
>
> Freeze-dried and/or dehydrated emergency food
>
> Seeds (wheat, corn, beans, etc.)
>
> Water purification pills, bottle of Clorox, and water filter system
>
> Animals for food: chickens, hogs, etc.
>
> Canning jars, paraffin
>
> Large cans to store beans, rice, etc.
>
> Buckets, pails and shovels
>
> Fishing equipment
>
> Water in storage containers

Other:

    Clothing
    Needles for sewing (many sizes), cloth
    Medicines: aspirin, cough syrup
    Chemical break-lights
    Matches and other fire starting equipment
    Toilet paper
    Boric acid
    Hydrogen Peroxide
    Painter's filter-mask, dust masks, goggles, hard hat
    Hand tools: axes, hammers (and nails), saws, hand planes, drills, files, grinder, etc.
    Camping type items: tent, lantern (and fuel), bed rolls, cots, stools, etc.
    Heavy duty cookware for use over a fire
    Drendle for making thread from wool
    Looms
    Hand grain and coffee grinder
    Pestels (hand grinding)
    Pens and paper
    Duct tape
    Air filters[1]

Energy generation equipment (some or all):

    Solar panels, battery bank and regulator
    Wind generator, battery bank and regulator
    Home distillation equipment
    Home hydrolysis equipment (separate hydrogen and oxygen from water)

---

[1]For safe area during the "three days of darkness"

Optional:

Hunting rifle (and bullets)
Bow and arrows
Welding equipment
Chain saw (gas or electric)
Animals: horses (or mules)
Bicycles and spare parts (chains, tires and tubes, repair
    kits)
Fire extinguishers
Pedal sewing machine
Food sealing machine
Motorcycle (and extra gas and oil)
Shell loading equipment
Air compressor
Telescope
Computer supplies (if have a computer)

Reference books to have on hand:

Boy Scout Fieldbook
How-to manuals on: tanning, baking bread, canning, can-
    dle making, animal care, soap making, etc.

3

Emergency Supplies

These are short-term emergency items. Some of these items will duplicate the "Items" list. This would be particularly helpful in a quick-escape emergency, such as violent weather. You might even want to organize these items into an "Emergency/Survival Kit."

Food—camping food, ready to eat, canned, etc. Include items like salt.

Bottled water and five gallon container of tap water, canteens

Clothing—especially for cold weather, boots and shoes, hats, rain gear, gloves.

Sleeping gear/bags, blankets, linens

First aid kit, including snake bite kit, treatment for chiggers and ticks, sunscreen lotion, betadine, hydrogen peroxide

Medicines, including Tylenol, Pepto Bismol, Kaopectate, cough syrup, hydrocortisone, topical ointment

Personal items—toothbrush, toothpaste, razor, shampoo, soap (antibacterial), comb or brush, extra eye glasses, personal medications, etc.

Ropes and balls of twine/cord

Tent(s), camp cots, camp chairs and tarp(s)

Camping stove and fuel

Camping lamp (and fuel), candles or oil lamps, chemical lightsticks

Camping utensils, can opener, drinking cups

Matches (in watertight container), butane lighter, magnesium fire starter

Bucket or water pails (for fire fighting, cleaning, drawing water, etc.

Flashlights (with fresh batteries)

Water purification tablets (or Clorox)

Toilet paper and Kleenex

Tools: shovel, axe/hatchet, handsaw, hammers, nails, screwdriver, screws, hand drill, files, pliers, socket wrenches, crescent wrenches, tin snips, chisels, crow bar, etc.

Knives, several types: hunting, butcher, paring

Whet stone (to sharpen knives)

Compass

Scissors

Trash bags

Transistor radio (with fresh battery)

Extra batteries

Whistle

Optional items:

CB walkie-talkies (pair)

Welder's goggles, painter's dust/filter mask, hard hat

4

References

Books (Prophesy):

Mary's Message to the World by Annie Kirkwood(1991). Blue Dolphin Publishing, PO Box 1908, Nevada City, CA 95959. ISBN 0-931892-66-X .

Mass Dreams of the Future by Chet B Snow, PhD and Helen Wambach, PhD. Sparrow Hawk Press, 11 Summit Ridge Drive, Tahlequah, OK 74464. ISBN 0-945027-08-7.

Rolling Thunder—The Coming Earth Changes by J. R. Jochmans (1980). Sun Publishing Company, PO Box 5588, Santa Fe, NM 87502-5588. ISBN 0-89540-058-8.

The Earth Changes Survival Handbook by Page Bryant (1983). Sun Publishing Company, PO Box 5588 Santa Fe, NM 87502-5588. ISBN 0-89540-150-9.

Black Dawn, Bright Day by Sun Bear with Wabun Wind (1990). Bear Tribe Publishing, PO Box 9167, Spokane, WA 99209-9167. ISBN 0-943404-18-5.

Upcoming Changes—The Next 20 Years by Joya Pope (1992). Emerald Wave Publishing Company, Box 969, Fayetteville, AR 72702. ISBN 0-942531-33-7.

Phoenix Rising—No-Eyes' Vision of the Changes to Come by Mary Summer Rain (1987). Schiffer Publishing Ltd., 1469 Morstein Road, West Chester, PA 199380.

Living is Forever by J. Edwin Carter (1990, 1992). Hampton Roads Publishing, 891 Norfolk Square, Norfolk, VA 23502, (804) 459-2453. This is a fictional story about the future earth changes containing a lot of spiritual truths and things to consider related to surviving.

Books (Communities)

Farms of Tomorrow—Community Supported Farms, Farm Supported Communities by Trauger M. Groh and Steven S.H. McFadden (1990). Bio-Dynamic Farming and Gardening Association Inc, PO Box 550, Kimberton, PA 19442. ISBN 0-938250-28.0.

Builders of the Dawn by Corrine McLaughlin and Gordon Davidson (1985). Sirius Publishing, Baker Rd, Shutesbury, MA 01072. ISBN 0-940-267-01-2.

Directory of Intentional Communities (1991). Co-published by Fellowship for Intentional Community, Evansville, IN and Communities Publications Cooperative, Rutledge, MO. ISBN 0-9602714-1-4.

Cohousing: A Contemporary Approach to Housing Ourselves by Kathryn McCamant & Charles Durrett. Ten Speed Press, PO Box 7123, Berkeley, CA 94707.

Books (Reference):

Producing Your Own Power—How to Make Nature's Energy Sources Work for You, edited by Carol Hupping Stoner (1975). Rodale Press. ISBN 0-87857-088-8.

Don't Waste Your Wastes—Compost 'em by Bert Whitehead (1991). Sunnyvale Press, PO Box 851971, Mesquite, TX 75185-1971. ISBN 0-9630612-0-8.

Hydroponics Soilless Gardening: The Beginner's Guide to Growing Vegetables, Houseplants, Flowers, and Herbs without Soil by Richard E. Nicholls (1977). Running Press, 125 S. Twenty-second St., Philadelphia, PA 19103. ISBN 0-89471-741-3.

Country Dreams—Your Guide to Saving Time and Money While Still Getting What You Want and Need in Country Property! (1991). Misty Mountain Press Inc, PO Box 210, Little Switzerland, NC 28749. Cost $12 postpaid.

Books (Survival/Emergency):

Family Emergency Plan (Volumes 1, 2 and 3) by Barry and Lynette Crockett, Publishers Press, Salt Lake City. These can be obtained from B & A Products for less than $10 per volume.

U.S. Army Survival Manual. Reprint of Department of the Army Field Manual FM21-76, Dorset Press, New York, 1992. To quote the preface of this book, "No one knows survival better than the U.S. Army, so this exceptional field guide is the most authoritative of its kind."

Magazines:

Practical Surviving. Mountain Star International, 1750 30th Street, Ste 498, Boulder, CO 80301, (303)449-4128.

Home Power Magazine. PO Box 520, Ashland, OR 97520, (916) 475-3179.

BackHome. WordsWorth Communications, Inc, 119 Third Ave West, Hendersonville, NC 28792.

Backwoods Home Magazine. 1257 Siskiyou Blvd #213, Ashland, OR 97520, (503)488-2053.

Newsletters:

"The Earth Changes Report" by Gordon-Michael Scallion, published monthly by Matrix Institute, RR1 Box 391, Westmoreland, NH 03467 (603)399-4916.

"Sparrow Hawk Villager," published by Light of Christ Community Church, Inc, 22 Summit Ridge Drive, Tahlequah, OK 74464-9215 (918)456-3421

"Rocky Mountain CoHousing Quarterly" is published by the Rocky Mountain CoHousing Association, 1705 14th Street #317, Boulder, CO 80302, (303)442-3280.

"Pamela's Pennypincher," 39 Green Meadow Blvd, Middletown, NJ 07748. $12.00 for 12 monthly issues.

"The Woodrew Update," Greta Woodrew and Dick Smolowe, 448 Rabbit Skin Road, Waynesville, NC 28786, (704) 926-3440 and FAX (704) 926-3445.

Catalogs/Information guides:

"1992 Planning Guide" by Backwoods Solar Electric Systems, 8530 Rapid Lightning Creek Rd, Sandpoint, ID 83864 (208)263-4290, owners Steve and Elizabeth Willey. This is an excellent "how-to" for solar power systems. It is a catalog of their products, but covers how to design your own system. Cost $3.00.

"Hydroponics Guidebook & Catalog," ECO Enterprises, 2821 NE 55th St, Seattle, WA 98105, (800)426-6937. Good overview of hydroponic and catalog. Cost $4.95.

"1992 Catalog No. 1. Energy Efficient Products, Independent Power Systems," Kansas Wind Power, Route 1, Holton, KS 66436, (913)364-4407. Cost $4.00.

Food and Preparedness catalog, NITRO-PAK Preparedness Center, 13309 Rosecrans Ave, Santa Fe Springs, CA 90670-4940, (310)802-0099.

Food supplier: Salt Lake Perma Pak, 230 East 6400 South, Murray, UT 84107, (801)268-9915.

Others:

"I AM AMERICA" map by Lori Wilkins, PO Box 2511, Payson, AZ 85547. Cost is $15 plus $3.00 for postage and handling.

Break lights and other survival items are available from: B&A Products, 2965 Country Place Circle, Carrollton, TX 75006, (214)416-0141 or fax (214)416-2141.

5

Update of Events Concerning the Predictions Chapter of Mary's Message

---

M ARY'S PREDICTIONS (CHAPTER 2) are not the main message of *Mary's Message to the World*, but they lend credibility to the seriousness of the message. The following is an update of the events that have happened since the book was finished and released to the publisher. These are a few of the events that we noticed through our narrow perspective of the world as viewed from information gained from our local newspapers (mostly *The Dallas Morning News* {DMN}) and watching the news on television (primarily CNN). It seems that I am adding items almost daily. To paraphrase the Eveready bunny TV commercial, the list "keeps on growing and growing and growing." As you read these items, please *note the dates* from the newspaper articles and other comments.

Timelines: the basic information was sent by Mary to Annie from 1987 to 1989. The compiling of the information was completed in July 1989. It was released to the publisher, Blue Dolphin Publishing, in Oct 1990, and we received our first two printed copies on May 22, 1991.

Miscellaneous mentions and quotes from the "Predictions" chapter in *Mary's Message to the World.*

WEATHER and STORMS:

... so will the winter season be unusual. There will be snowfall in places which have not often had snow. (p9)

Weather patterns will change dramatically all over the world. The winter months will be colder and in many areas wetter. (p7)

The storms will come slowly and grow each year. The days of cloudiness will increase erratically. At times when you need rain, there will be none. When it does rain, it will come in too great of quantities and too many days at a time. (pp24-25)

Last winter (1990-91) Southern California experienced one of the coldest winters. This spring (1991) there were many floods. CNN reported that Louisiana had had 32 straight days of rain.

(DMN, p7A, Tuesday, June 19, 1990, "'90 weather among worst in years") "Nature appears to have unleashed one of its worst weather tantrums in four decades ..."

(DMN, front page, Friday, November 8, 1991, "Philippine typhoon's ravages assessed")

(The Hemet News [Hemet, Calif], front page, August 15, 1992, "Summer storm strikes Valley") "Swirling, monsoon-like showers, accompanied by crackling bolts of lightning, raged through the Valley late Friday afternoon ..."

(San Francisco Chronicle, Saturday, September 5, 1992, "EARTH WEEK/A weekly diary of the planet" by Steve Newman.) "**Killing Snow**—Farmers in New Zealand's South Island suffered huge losses as severe storms brought heavy snowfall for the second time within a month. The fierce storm killed thousands of newborn lambs and many of the sheep that had survived the previous storm ... **Floods**—At least 80 people were drowned and more than two million displaced by flash floods which swept across parts of India's Orissa state. The inundations swamped crops and houses and led epidemics of cholera and gastroenteritis. Heavy flooding was also reported in eastern Sudan and in Adelaide, Australia."

(DMN, p5A, Tuesday, September 15, 1992, "Around the World—Pakistan government orders flood evacuation") "KARACHI, Pakistan—The government ordered the evacuation of half a million people in southern Pakistan on Monday, bracing for more flooding . . . At least 650 people died in heavy rain and flash floods . . . newspapers put the death toll as high as 1,800 . . ."

(DMN, p18A, Monday, October 19, 1992, "Around the World—Storms kill 7 in Mexico, leave hundreds homeless") "MEXICO CITY—Seven people have died in two days of fierce rainstorms in Atizapan de Zaragosa in Mexico . . . The storms, which unleashed 6-foot-high floodwaters, damaged more than 300 homes and left 1,600 people homeless . . ."

*The **ocean currents** are now churning and just beginning to change their direction. The **British Islands** will most likely be the first to notice the changing currents. The people of these isles will experience much wetness and more cold than usual. (pp9-10)*

(DMN, p18A, Saturday, January 27, 1990, "94 die as storm slashed across Western Europe") "Hardest hit was **Britain**, where 45 people were reported killed . . ."

1990-1992: Your government leaders will be getting the messages of some unusual occurrences in the tidal flows. The oceans will begin to churn and there will be evidence of changing patterns in the way currents flow. (p12)

(DMN, p3F, Monday, August 3, 1992, "Turning down summer's heat") ". . . says this summer will probably end up being the coolest in years. A volcanic eruption in the Philippines last year may be the cause of the cooler weather. And **shifting ocean currents** off the west coast of South America may be cooling things off a bit, too."

*. . . the sky will begin to darken and there will be more rains than usual. The so-called "**greenhouse** effect" will multiply its effects on earth. As the **volcanos** add new ash and debris to the upper atmosphere . . . (p24)*

(DMN, p3F, Monday August 3, 1992, "Turning down summer's heat") "But a **volcano** such as Mount Pianatubo produces a lot of sulfur dioxide. In the stratosphere the sulfur dioxide is converted to sulfuric acid, which combines with water to form tiny droplets. The droplets intercept sunlight, sending a small percentage of the sun's energy back into space. Scientists at the Goddard Institute incorporate this into their **greenhouse** warming model."

You have just begun to see the fury of these storms. Those which come in 1990 and 1991, even though they will be of an increased size, will be nothing in comparison to the future storms which will lash the globe. (p22)

Over 100,000 people died in April/May 1991 in Bangladesh.

Hurricane Andrew hit Florida and Louisiana August 24-26, 1992. DMN Aug 30, 1992 front page "Andrew may be century's most destructive storm." DMN Aug 30, 1992, p31A "Andrew may signal chaotic future—Forecasters predict increase in storms, fear logistical nightmares."

(DMN, front page, Sunday, September 13, 1992, "Hurricane pounds Hawaiian island") (DMN, front page, Monday, September 14, 1992 "Cleanup begins after Hawaii storm") "Hurricane Iniki, the **strongest hurricane to hit Hawaii this century ... 10,000 homes were badly damaged and crops were ruined ... with 130-mph sustained wind and gusts of up to 160 mph.**"

*There will also be **floods**, **mud slides**, and **torrential rains** ... (p13)*
... other parts of the world will be experiencing major earthquakes and **mud slides**. *(p14)*

(DMN, p23A, June 6, 1991, "Around the World — Rains trigger **landslides** in Colombia, killing 46") "BOGOTA, Colombia — Two landslides caused by **torrential rains** in the Andes mountains killed 46 people ..."

(DMN, p12A, June 19, 1991, "Chilean mudslide kills at least 64") "ANTOFAGASTA, Chile—A **mudslide** slammed into hillside slums in this northern desert city ... rare **torrential rains** ... one of the most arid areas of the world."

(DMN, p10A, Friday, July 12, 1991, "China requests aid to help it cope with months of flooding") "BEIJING—The government appealed for the first time for foreign aid in a disaster Thursday, seeking help to cope with **floods** that have killed more than 1,200 people since January and left millions homeless . . . Meteorologists predicted no break in the heavy rains . . ."

(DMN, front page, Saturday, July 13, 1991, picture titled "Flooding besets China") ". . . more than 40 inches of rain since May"

(DMN, p8A, Sunday, February 16, 1992, "Fierce, fast storm hits S. California" ". . . **Mudslides** threatened homes . . . throughout the historical series of storms."

(DMN, p20A, Thursday, September 14, 1992, "Around the World—France's deadliest storm in 34 years kills at least 30")

*There will be **tornados** in areas where there have never been tornados.*
(p12)

(DMN front page, November 23, 1992, "Tornadoes, storms kill 24 in South")

(DMN, p24A, November 23, 1992, "Harris residents clean up after tornadoes")

((DMN, p4A, November 24, 1992, "Tornadoes in NC kill 2, toss bus off road, smash homes") "Other deaths from the **unusual** November thunderstorm system include . . ."

*Many **new records will be set**, many unusual events will be reported.*
(p10)

(DMN p9A, Saturday, June 1, 1991, "Tornado warnings ignored") "The 1,182 tornadoes reported last year in the continental United States **set a record** for the forty years that the weather service has kept track, said Jim Henderson, deputy director of the service's National Severe Storms Forecast Center in Kansas City, Mo."

(DMN, p7A, Saturday, June 1, 1991, "Lingering heat wave sizzles Eastern states") "The heat **broke records** in parts of Virginia and Pennsylvania."

(DMN, p9A, Sunday, November 3, 1991, "Record cold follows snow in Midwest") "**Record** cold Saturday followed record snowfall in the Midwest . . . At least seven weather-related deaths have been reported . . ."

(DMN, p33A, Friday, December 20, 1991, "Area may break record for yearly rainfall") "As the rain fell Thursday, a 59-year old weather **record** came close to falling, too." "'We're in a wet pattern now,' Mr Moller said. 'It's **unusual**, especially at this time of year.'"

(DMN, p3A, Monday, March 9, 1992, "Winter brought **record** warmth") "In the 97 years Uncle Sam has been keeping records, never has a winter been so warm as this December, January and February, the National Climatic Data Center says."

(DMN, p3A, Tuesday, June 23, 1992, "Cold weather sets **records** in 18 states") "The second full day of summer dawned Monday like the last day of winter, with record low temperatures as low as the 30s from the Mississippi Valley to the East Coast . . ."

(DMN, p8A, Wednesday, June 24, 1992, "Around the World —Extreme heat kills at least 6 in northern Mexico") ". . . three days after a **record** high of 117 was recorded in one desert town . . ."

(The Plain Dealer [Cleveland, Ohio], front page, July 31, 1992, "Noah, it's not getting any better—July storms bring the area **record** rainfall") "The wettest July on record has been a month of flooded houses, fallen trees, blocked roads, downed power lines and flaring tempers."

(unknown newspaper, Wednesday, July 8, 1992, p8A, "Rare tornado stuns Panama, kills nine") ". . . The storm, carrying winds of more than 150 mph, was the first confirmed tornado recorded in Panama . . ."

(San Luis Obispo County TELEGRAM-TRIBUNE, Aug 1992, "July one of coldest on **record**")

The droughts which are affecting the world will continue. Those who reside on the African continent will be most affected, but other parts of the world will also begin to feel the droughts. The middle part of Russia will have floods and rains which will be unequalled in their damage. (p11)

(DMN p22A, Wednesday, June 17, 1992, "Around the World— 5,000 children are dying daily in Somalia's drought")

But some of the scientists will come out in favor of having research to study the changing patterns around the globe. (p12)

EARTHQUAKES:

*Mary's prediction is that the next major event will be an **earthquake in Italy**. (p9)*

*Also there will be **earthquakes in Italy**. (p11)*
In May 1991 CNN reported an **earthquake in Southern Italy** that was 4.6 on the Richter scale. (Note: this was not the big one.)

The earthquakes will begin in this manner. There have already been several of large intensity in recent months. Each round of earthquake activity

will progress in intensity and frequency. The amount of damage will grow.
(p24)

(DMN, front page, Monday, June 25, 1990, "Toll rises to 50,000 in Iran") "The most powerful aftershock in three days rocked earthquake-devastated northern Iran on Sunday, triggering a landslide that blocked the road linking this shattered city to the Caspian Sea coast. The casualty toll climbed to 50,000 killed and 200,000 wounded . . ."

July 5, 1991, CNN told of an earthquake in Indonesia that measured 6.3 on the Richter scale.

July 14, 1991, CNN announced that an earthquake was reported in Pakistan that measured 6.6 on the Richter scale.

(DMN, p11A, Sunday, February 16, 1992, "Around the World—Thousands flee likely volcanic eruption near Manila" "MANILA, Philippines - Thousands of people began fleeing a volcanic island south of Manila . . . Scientists recorded 406 rock-fracturing quakes during a 29-hour period . . ."

(DMN, p21A, Saturday, March 14, 1992, "Quake rocks eastern Turkey - Over 570 people killed; large part of 1 city reduced to rubble")

(DMN, p10A, Tuesday, April 14, 1992, "Around the World—Rare earthquake rattles northern Europe, injuring 45") "HEINSBERG, Germany—A rare and powerful earthquake . . . to 6.3 at Germany's Seismological Central Observatory in Erlangen . . . that would make it the strongest quake in the region in more than 200 years."

(San Francisco Chronicle, August 20, 1992, "20 Feared Dead in Kyrgyzstan Quake") "Moscow—A powerful earthquake on the border of China and Kyrgyzstan devastated at least one village early yesterday and killed up to 20 people . . . measured 7.5 on the Richter scale . . ."

(DMN, p20A, Thursday, September 3, 1992, "Nicaragua tidal waves kill 60—Thousands homeless in disaster unleashed by quake") This tidal wave was caused by a 7.0 earthquake. Waves reached a height of 45 feet.

(DMN, p7a, Thursday, Sept 3, 1992, "Around the U.S.—Moderate quake rattles part of Utah") This was a 5.5 earthquake that closed Zion National Park.

*The earthquakes, which will begin on the **Eastern seaboard of America**, will take place infrequently. There will be small tremors this winter in the northeast of your country. (p11)*

(DMN, p5A, Tuesday, June 18, 1991, "Around the U.S.— **Eastern states shaken** by minor earthquake") "ALBANY, N.Y. —A minor earthquake centered 40 miles west of here rattled parts of New York, Massachusetts and Connecticut before dawn Monday. The tremor, which measured 3.9 on the Richter scale, hit at 4:53 a.m. and lasted less than 10 seconds, the U.S. Geological Survey said."

(San Francisco Chronicle, Aug 22, 1992 pA5, "Noisy Earthquake Rattles South Carolina Coast") This tells about an earthquake measuring 4.1 on the Richter scale centered about 20 miles north-north-west of Charleston.

(San Francisco Chronicle, September 16, 1992, "60% Chance of Quake in N.Y.") "New York—New York has a 60 percent chance of suffering a major earthquake that could cause as much as $25 billion in damage, a team of civil engineers said yesterday . . ."

In 1990, other earthquakes will be felt in Central America. **Peru will** *have a major earthquake in the mountainous areas and it will cause much loss of life. But this is only the beginning. (p11)* (Note: this was received in the message given on July 19, 1988.)

(DMN, 7A, Friday, June 1, 1990, "Aftershocks rattle Peruvian towns, terrifying survivors") "TARAPOTO, Peru—Dozens of strong aftershocks rocked jungle villages Thursday in northern **Peru**, and terrified people crowded into town squares, fearful their homes would collapse on them if another killer quake occurred. At least 135 people died when an earthquake measuring 6.3 on the Richter scale struck the area about 400 miles north of Lima late Tuesday . . ."

(DMN, same page and day, "Quake hits Mexico; no injuries reported") ". . . measured the quake at 6.1 on the open-ended Richter scale."

(Friend's Review, Vol 3 Issue 2 - Jun 1991- Summer) *Mary's Message* was reviewed by Berdell Moffett. Here is a quote from that review, "as I was reading *Mary* predicting the changes that would be taking place on the earth, I came to a passage that talks of forthcoming earthquakes in Peru. As I was reading this, and questioning the validity of that prediction, a newscaster broke into the programming on my radio and announced a **serious earthquake in Peru**. Woooooooow!"

(DMN, p6A, Tuesday, May 26, 1992, "Strong earthquake injures 40 in Cuba") "HAVANA—A strong earthquake . . . measured 6.9 on the Richter scale."

Although there may not be anything unusual about earthquakes in California, I thought I would still track some of the reports we received.

(DMN, 7A, Saturday, June 29, 1991, "Quake hits LA area; 2 killed—Dozens are injured in foothill suburbs") "SIERRA MADRE, Calif—A strong earthquake rolled through Southern California on Friday . . . The tremor measured 6.0 on the Richter scale . . . on the Sierra Madre Fault . . . The fault had not produced a sizable quake in 10,000 years."

(DMN, p4A, Saturday, July 6, 1991, "Around the World—No injuries reported in moderate S. California quake") ". . . The 4.0-magnitude quake was centered near Castaic, about 40 miles northwest of downtown Los Angeles . . ."

(DMN, p9A, Saturday, April 25, 1992, "Wednesday quake was largest in lower 48 states since 1989") "The earthquake that jolted Southern California this week was the largest in the lower 48 states . . ."

(DMN, front page, Monday, June 29, 1992, "Strongest quake in years jars California") This is about the two earthquakes in California measuring 7.4 and 6.5 on the Richter scale that happened Sunday. Monday a 5.4 happened 70 miles north of Las Vegas, NV.

(DMN, p7A, Friday, July 10, 1992, "Around the U.S.—16 injured in quake aftershock") This is about the aftershocks in Big Bear Lake, California, measuring 5.5 on the Richter scale.

Other miscellaneous earthquakes:

(DMN, p6A, Saturday, July 13, 1991, "Around the U.S.— Strong offshore quake shakes Oregon cities") "PORTLAND, Ore—. . . The quake registered 6.6 on the Richter scale . . . 'We would call it a major earthquake.'"

(DMN, p8A, Saturday, March 21, 1992, "Around the U.S. . . . Briefly" "An earthquake measuring 4.1 on the Richter scale shook western Montana on Friday evening and was felt in Ovando, Helena, and Great Falls . . ."

VOLCANOS:

There will be increases in the frequency and activity of earthquakes and volcanos ... (p7)

Volcanos will come out of nowhere. **Old volcanos will become active** *and alive with fury. (p22)*

The volcanos have already commenced ... As the time draws near, other volcanos will begin to flow and spill much lava and create new ground ... As **the volcanos add new ash and debris to the upper atmosphere,** *the land will be under siege from storms. (p24)*

More **earthquakes** *will be felt, but perhaps not as severely as the ones before.* **Japan** *will continue to feel the earth as it trembles and moves. It will shake loose Japan's power center and they will be caring for their own and will not be able to take advantage of the world situation for gain. (p16)*

Japan *will fall into the sea and that part of the world will become frozen wasteland. (p20)*

(DMN, front page, Tuesday, June 4, 1991, "**Volcano erupts in Japan—Up to 12 people killed; dozens missing**") "**Black volcanic ash from Mount Unzen blocks out the sky** Monday over Shimabara, in southern Japan." "TOKYO—A volcano in southwestern Japan erupted late Monday, killing as many as 12 people, setting houses and forest aflame and raining superheated rocks on small villages . . . appeared to be among the **largest** volcanic eruptions in Japan in at least half a century . . . The area was jolted by **11 earthquakes** during the night . . ."

(DMN, p13A, June 7, 1991, "Eruption a reminder of 1792 disaster—Japan wary as latest explosion of lava, gases extends it reach.") "No matter how economically powerful **Japan** seems from the outside, it is taken as accepted wisdom here, that **the country is a fragile island, constantly subject to natural and manmade destruction.**"

(DMN, p16A, June 9, 1991, "Volcano erupts anew in Japan; homes burn") "Japan's Mount Unzen belches ash, hot gas and molten rock Saturday in its second eruption in less than a week."

(DMN, front page and p11A, June 10, 1991, "Philippine volcano forces evacuation of U.S. base") "MANILA, Philippines—The U.S. military on Monday began evacuating thousands of Americans from Clark Air Base after a nearby volcano that **had been dormant for centuries** spewed rocks and ash down its slopes . . . The volcanoes rumbling in Japan and the Philippines belong to the Ring of Fire circling the Pacific, but **their simultaneous eruptions appear to be mere coincidence**, experts said Friday."

(DMN, p20A, June 13, 1991, "Volcano erupts again—Philippines blast called biggest yet") ". . . 'What we are seeing now are phenomenal eruptions,' said Raymundo Punongbayan, director of the Philippine Institute of Vulcanology and Seismology."

(DMN, p8A, June 19, 1991, "Volcano paralyzes area of Philippines") "... More than a week of eruptions from Mount Pinatubo ... have coated the surrounding area with ash and triggered cascades of mud and sand ... The Red Cross has reported at least 146 deaths."

(DMN, front page, Saturday, April 11, 1992, "Nicaraguan volcano erupts") "A boy surveys the plume of volcanic debris rising Friday from the Cerro Negro volcano, northwest of Managua, Nicaragua. The eruption Thursday forced the evacuation of thousands of villagers."

(DMN, p6A, Sunday, June 28, 1992, "Around the U.S.— Alaska volcano dormant 39 years spews ash, steam") "The Mount Spurr volcano ended 39 years of dormancy Saturday ..."

(San Francisco Chronicle, August 19, 1992, "Volcano spews ash over Anchorage") "... The volcano, about 80 miles west of Anchorage, erupted Tuesday for the second time this summer, spewing ash more than 10 miles into the sky ... Police warned drivers to stay off the roads because of reduced visibility and the chances of losing control on the slick coat of volcanic ash."

THE UNIVERSE and SPACE DEBRIS:

The universe is growing and expanding *and will soon explode in new growth and new life. It is as though the whole universe has been pregnant for many hundreds of years. (p20)*

(DMN, p6D, Monday, March 25, 1991, "Discoveries—Science Update—New analysis supports view that universe is expanding") "Measurements of the brightness of distant galaxies support the standard view that **the universe is expanding,** a new analysis has found."

The wave of new and different energy which is approaching the planet is bringing with it much debris from outer space. The debris will cause lights to flash in the atmosphere. Some of the debris will land on Earth causing craters and changes to Earth's lands. (p25)

(DMN, p7A, Friday, January 25, 1991, "Around The U.S.—Rare asteroid approach surprises astronomers") "Astronomers scanning the sky a week ago were astonished to see a small asteroid streaking by Earth, within less than half the distance to the Moon. It was the smallest, closest asteroid ever observed passing safely by Earth . . ."

(DMN, front page, Tuesday, June 18, 1991, "Asteroid concerns gaining credence—Experts study threat of 'killer' rock") ". . . Last year Congress called for a series of detailed studies after a half-mile-wide asteroid crossed Earth's path at an uncomfortably close distance in 1989."

There will be comets which will come through your solar system. (p15)
(DMN p6D, Monday, January 22, 1990, "Discoveries—Science Update—Recently discovered **comet** may glimmer in late April sky")

(The New York Times, pA12, Wednesday, September 30, 1992, "After 130-year Absence, A Comet Reappears") "**Comet** Swift-Tuttle, which produces Earth's spectacular Perseid meteor shower every August, has been spotted for the first time in 130 years, astronomers said today."

SUN ACTIVITY and SOLAR FLARES:

*There will be reports of **unusual** sun activity. (p10)*

The sun will also contribute to the destruction by performing in ways to which your scientists are not accustomed. (p23)
(DMN, p6D, Monday, June 24, 1991, "Discoveries—Silent storm—This month's solar turbulence playing havoc with Earth's communications, power systems") "Unlike hurricanes or blue northers, with their tree-bending gales and drenching downpours, the geomagnetic storms that have been sweeping across the Earth this month are largely silent and invisible. Yet storms they are . . . The nearly unbroken spate of geomagnetic disturbance on Earth since June 1 'is **unusual**,' said Joseph Allen of the National Geophysical Data Center in Boulder, Colorado."

FOREST FIRES:

The forest fires have just begun . . . (p23)
In May 1991, CNN reported about the huge forest fire in Alaska.
June 30, 1991, CNN reported on Canada's largest forest fire in Quebec covering 600,000 acres.

(DMN, p3A, Monday, August 3, 1992, "Firefighters work to contain blaze spreading near Yosemite")

(San Francisco Chronicle, Satuday, September 12, 1992, "EARTH WEEK/A weekly diary of the planet" by Steve Newman.) "Wildfires—Fires raging northeast of Athens were brought under control after destroying almost 15,000 acres of Greek pine forests. Numerous forest fires also broke out on the Mediterranean island of Corsica. In the western United States, cool and rainy weather slowed wildfires burning in Idaho's national forest on terrain parched by six years of drought. Nearly 600,000 acres of forest has been blackened in Idaho this year."

OTHER:

World hunger will be increasing . . . (p 10)
This is happening now (Spring/Summer 1991) in Africa, and the news mentions it almost daily.
(unknown newspaper, August 1992, "Rural Somalis dying at rate of 2,000 a day, officals say")

In the news during this year, there will begin to be predictions about the coming events. There will be many who still doubt. But some of the scientists will come out in favor of having research to study the changing patterns around the globe. Countries which have been hostile to each other will begin dialogue on this all important topic. (1990-1992 p 12)
(DMN, front page, Thursday, June 4, 1992, "Earth Summit opens with pleas for planet—U.N. chief asks for halt in rivalries")

MARY'S APPARITIONS:

I am appearing throughout the world. I will continue to appear in many diverse places. These apparitions will be for the sole purpose of warning you of the times ahead. (p3)
Mary will increase her apparitions throughout the world. (p7)

I will be appearing in many places in these next few years. If my apparitions increase, perhaps the general population will take notice and question. (p27)

(San Francisco Chronicle, pA3, Saturday, December 8, 1990, "Pilgrims Jam Gold-Rush Town for 'Vision'—The image some say is the Virgin Mary clogs traffic and boosts business in tiny Colfax") ". . . St. Dominic's Church, where 5,000 pilgrims waited yesterday to glimpse what some are calling an apparition of the Virgin Mary."

The story about Mother Mary appearing in Medjugorje, Yugoslavia is no new news. But what is significant is that *Life* magazine has picked up on it in their July 1991 issue. The front cover of the magazine is titled "Do You Believe In Miracles? If you do, you're not alone. From a vision of the Virgin Mary on a hillside in Yugoslavia to the face of Christ on a billboard in Georgia, signs of a divine presence are touching millions."

June 24, 1991 our local channel 4 news had a special on Mary's appearances in Yugoslavia.

(The Denver Post, p1A, 10A, 11A, 13A, Sunday, December 8, 1991, "Shrine prepares for thousands of worshipers" and "Are they real? Skeptics, believers discuss apparitions" and "Visionary 'overwhelmed' by sightings") These discuss Mary's appearance to Theresa Lopez in Colorado. She has seen Mary eight times.

(Atlanta Journal, June 15, 1992, Tom Murphy, "Religion, CONYERS: Virgin Mary crowd doubles.") "The crowds that gather to hear what Conyers resident Nancy Fowler says are her monthly messages from the Virgin Mary . . ."

(unknown paper 'Sun,' "Woman claims image is of the Virgin Mary") "San Bernardino residents Sally Menor, Lucy Rangel and Margarita Guzman pray in front of a tree they say contains the image of Our Lady of Guadalupe on a knot (of a tree) ... The tree is in the 1400 block of Turrill Avenue in San Bernardino."

(San Francisco Chronicle, June 23, 1992, "Pilgrims Flock to Watsonville Oak Tree—Faithful claim to see Virgin of Guadalupe's outline on bark")

(The Hemet [CA] News, Aug 3, 1992, "Thousands seek vision of Mary") "MARLBORO, NJ—Almost 7,000 people gathered in a man's back yard to wait for a vision of the Virgin Mary . . ."

San Francisco Examiner, Sept 1, 1992, "That vision of the Virgin Mary: some pilgrims say she appeared") "COLD SPRING, Ky—Thousands drawn by a mystic's reported prediction that an apparition would appear here at midnight Monday flocked to a small-town church, and some said they had seen the Virgin Mary appear in a pine tree."

(DMN, p6A, Monday, September 7, 1992, "Around the U.S.—
Some claim to feel Virgin Mary's presence in NJ yard")

(DMN, p5F, Sunday, October 18, 1992, "Sightings of Mary have
increased sharply," by James D. Davis, Fort Lauderdale Sun-Sentinel.)

**Specializing in Spiritual
Advancement and Emergency/
Survival Products**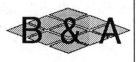

B & A Products is devoted to carrying high quality products for Spiritual Advancement and Emergency/ Survival. These include:

Books
Spiritual enlightenment, earth changes, prophesy, reference material, survival books

Food
Emergency food (MREs) and long-term storage food

Supplies
Break lights, hard hats, dust masks, goggles, first-aid kits, 72-hour emergency kits, long lasting candles, portable water containers, water purification tablets, waterproof matches, emergency blankets, camping gear, tools

Specialty Items
Solar powered devices

We will be adding items as we get calls for them

For the current catalog and price list, contact:
B & A Products — 2965 Country Place Circle
Carrollton, TX 75006
Call (214) 416-0141 or Fax (214) 416-2141